WISDOM OF THE HAND

A Guide to the Jazz Pentatonic Scales

by Marius Nordal

Music Engraving - Robert Puff and Larry Dunlap
Cover Design - John Bishop and Linda McLaughlin

ISBN 1-883217-84-9

For Alicia and Susan

And in memory of Drs. Martin Mailman and Leon Breeden who sit as a silent tribunal, watching over my every creative move.

With a special thank you to my life-long piano teacher, Jerome Gray, Zen master of the three-word music lesson. In 50 years, I've only been able absorb the tiniest portion of his genius.

Table of Contents

Part IV - The Blues Scales

Part V - The Amazing 88 Note Scale

Part VI - The Coltrane Pentatonic Scale

Part VII - The Major Flatted-6th Pentatonic Scale

Part VIII - Creativity

Part IX - Chordal vs. Linear Improvising

Part X - Coda

Preface - **What's in This Book**

The original idea for this book was for it to be a tutorial on how to finger the major and minor pentatonic scales over several octaves. But as things unfolded, that limited approach appeared like it might only lead to an end product that wasn't much more than an extended typing lesson on the piano. There are many books like that already on the market and one more volume would just contribute to the inflationary spiral. That definitely was not of the grand and useful scale that I had envisioned.

I suddenly wanted to put together something that would not only be lucid but inspiring too. I wanted to excite pianists by not only exploring those areas that they didn't know much about but those they had never even heard of.

Thus, over time, the book expanded into many areas of music knowledge beyond scale fingerings. These include chapters covering The Amazing 88 Note Scale, Rhythmic Creativity, Escaping Major 7th Hell, Positional Playing, Big Hand/Small Hand, Octave Bending and What Instrument is a Piano?

The unifying philosophy here is that everything presented should be something that the hand can really use. For what is in a pianist's hand dictates what is improvised as much as the head does. In the end, I now see that the entire book boils down to two simple technical concepts: positional playing and what I call making a "small hand."

The ultimate goal (other than perhaps learning some of the pieces for pleasure and enjoyment) is for you to break away from all your standard licks before you end up just quoting them verbatim because that's all your hand knows! This will be done by drastically increasing the pathways for the hand to travel through so it can always be "on its way" somewhere. To that end, rhythm will be discussed too. The joy and beauty of freely being able to travel through all 24 major and minor keys is that the varied geography of the various keys produces different music. And you will not freeze up any more when the bridge of a song suddenly goes to the key of B or F#!

These are the things that make us play and sound smarter then we really are.

This is the opulent stuff we dream about playing but wake up the next morning to find that we can't recall a single note of it.

These are the things you wildly grab for, quickly run out of gas in about eight measures and then sadly return to the old sorry way you were trying to escape from in the first place!

Every aspect and topic is fully explained and also backed up with detailed explanations showing how things are done. This is accomplished via 235 exercises and 45 etudes.

VIDEO LESSONS

Much of the material in this book is compiled from the 60 jazz lessons posted on You Tube under either Marius Nordal or the handle radiokid2. Selected examples of those are listed on page 253 in this book.

Introduction - **Conquering Space**

The world of jazz and pop music is so over-populated with amazing, virtuoso guitarists and horn players that we poor keyboard players can sometimes develop a technical inferiority complex. Who hasn't heard a face-melting saxophone solo by someone like Charlie Parker or Michael Brecker and felt that only the greatest keyboard geniuses could ever equal that? An unhappy reality is that, while most instruments can cover two or more octaves while barely moving their hands, we pianists spend our lives negotiating through a swath of keys four feet wide…and we can't even see both ends at the same time! The pentatonic scales make things especially challenging for us because there are so few notes in an octave.

Thought Experiment

Try to imagine a piano with all of the white keys removed: all that would be left would be a few black keys spread out over four feet of empty space! Traditional fingerings wouldn't work very well and your hand would keep slipping off the keys into your lap quite a bit. If this is what you've been experiencing while attempting to play the pentatonic scales or perhaps the way you feel about your keyboard playing in general, then this is the book for you. It contains a wealth of information that will enable you to conquer the vast empty spaces across the pentatonic terrain, plus it presents various mental and technical tricks that will help you become more creative too.

When I was playing in blues bands in high school, we played all sorts of soul music, blues and early rock 'n' roll which are all largely based on the major and minor pentatonic scales. I remember being fascinated by these five notes and sensed that there was a whole galaxy of stuff in them to be accessed. All of the emotionally rich music we were playing seemed to be just scratching the surface of something much greater that pianists just weren't accessing on the keyboard yet. I couldn't even begin to unlock the real potential until a few years later when I first heard McCoy Tyner and early Chick Corea. Back then, as now, nobody seemed to know any good fingerings or could get much beyond playing little, repeated sequences of three and four note patterns, thus we all just imitated what was being done by the masters. This book is will attempt to solve many of those problems that have been bugging keyboard players for decades.

There's lots of territory covered in these pages as they range through scales, technique, etudes, rhythms, music philosophy and even a few jokes now and then. In fact, it might appear that there are several books here, all rolled into one. So, if you have a special interest in a particular scale or concept, feel free to skip ahead and divide your attention between several chapters at once.

Part I: Pentatonic Challenges

"That's the beauty of the piano: the different geography of the various keys produces different music."

Before you dig into the pentatonic scales, we'll take a look at how their keyboard geography is an alien concept to the European-oriented keyboard tradition.

Chapter 1 - Three Keyboard Challenges

Challenge #1: Positional Playing, Traveling and Avoiding the "Thumb Under" Syndrome.

The first major challenge that pianists face is moving large distances around the keyboard. The instant you rest your hands on the keys, you're locked into a one octave "box." Any switch to a higher or lower octave involves a clumsy, thumb-under move or a sudden, flying, circus leap that extends all the way from the shoulder to the fingertips. If you don't feel comfortable "traveling," then you may end up sending away a whole world of music and get stuck playing in a very narrow range while the rest of your keyboard literally collects dust. You know who you are out there…go grab a dust rag right now and take a look at the highest and lowest octave on your piano!

To enable easy traveling through the wider intervals and weird geography of the pentatonic scales, we'll be trying out some unorthodox fingerings that will avoid crossing the thumb under as much as possible. I call this positional playing. The thumb will transport the hand to a new position on the keys and the music will be conceived in little groups of three or four notes until it's time to jump to the next position. You can play just about every two-octave scale in this book in just three positions! This will often involve the "forbidden" use of the thumb on the black keys.

KEITH SPEAKS

I once did an interview with Keith Jarrett for *Jazz Times* magazine and he made an interesting comment that I now realize was about this concept of positional playing. He said that a knowledgeable pianist came up after a concert and observed that Keith seemed to use very unorthodox fingerings during his most creative moments. He told Jarrett "The only thing I can figure out is, whatever is happening is faster than your ability to come up with logical fingerings." Jarrett's comment on that was "I told him he was exactly right."

Since that interview I've come to understand that Keith Jarrett tends to conceive of music in little handfuls of three or four notes. They aren't always the same groupings that are used in the pentatonic scales but the principle is the same. He has an infinite supply of little chord shapes that he breaks into single notes and moves about the keyboard, thus mostly avoiding the problem of constantly turning his thumb under. McCoy Tyner also does exactly the same thing.

The important point here is that if a cornerstone of this book's philosophy is that of positional playing, then it's vital to understand that the thumb is the navigator, the locater and your guide for transporting the entire arm to be in a perfect spot to play that next handful of keys.

The payoff here is that, even though positional playing won't guarantee you a good night on a gig, I can assure you that you will never have a bad night. That's because all the scales and etudes presented here tend to make the 24 major and minor keys more equal. That way you won't have to panic anymore when the bridge of an "easy" song suddenly modulates to a scary key like F# or B!

> ## *HOW MUCH IS THE THUMB USED IN PENTATONIC SCALES?*
>
> *I actually counted how many times various fingers are used when playing all twelve pentatonic scales. The winners were the thumb and index fingers, each tied at 26%. In other words, when added together those two fingers are playing slightly more than half of all the notes. This just confirms that training those two members of the digit family to become useful is vital in negotiating the widely spaced pentatonic intervals. It will also allow the hand to be freer and feed new tactile moves into your brain so it can be more creative too.*

Challenge #2: Discard Those Old, Single Octave Fingerings

The second keyboard challenge concerns one of the most neglected and misunderstood areas in modern piano technique: that of finding some decent fingerings for the pentatonic and blues scales. Keyboards were invented in Europe centuries ago and all the major and minor scales from that culture had notes that lay conveniently right next to each other. This resulted in a nice, neat, twelve-note, one-octave fingering scheme. Since then, pianists have always been trained to try to solve all scale fingerings within that one octave… it's an ingrained, cultural prejudice. But the pentatonic scale contains only five notes, which creates some wide intervals for the hand to deal with. What to do? The answer: we'll use a two-octave fingering.

Say what? Yes, you read that correctly, two-octave fingerings do exist! In the first applied section of this book (Chapter Three) we'll start by laying out all twelve minor pentatonic scale fingerings for both hands and include little jazz etudes for you to practice on. The very first scale will be E flat minor, which is on the five black keys. This will cultivate accuracy because any flaws will cause your fingers (especially the thumb) to slip right off the keys just like a drunk trying to walk on a balance beam!

POSITIONAL PLAYING AND THE THUMB

Like most players, you've probably been told to avoid using the thumb on a black key whenever possible, but positional playing is *defined* by where the thumb lands. Discouraging the use of black keys as landing spots sends away 5 out of 12 creative options!

Conventional wisdom says that if you have a choice then, sure, avoid using the thumb. Hey, let's face it, that clumsy little midget that protrudes from the arm can barely even reach the black keys. In fact, back in Bach's day, they only used four fingers and tried to avoid using the thumb altogether! But times have changed and these days the thumb and index finger pretty much rule the hand.

Really? That's right. In theory, you should be able to play scales only as fast as your thumb can guide your hand to the next keyboard position. Keep in mind that the thumb is not a "finger," it's an extension of the arm, which is probably the reason it has a different name. The remaining four fingers are just little flippers that twitch around the keyboard after they've been transported there by the thumb, which acts as a guide for the entire arm. The heart of playing all the scales and ideas presented here is not to avoid the thumb but to learn how to effectively use it on the black keys, which is something that piano teachers usually don't recommend. But, then again, most piano teachers are very Eurocentric and don't improvise. They have the luxury of spending months poring over old music and choreographing the cool keyboard moves created by composers who did improvise.

THUMB SECRETS

So, what is the secret of good thumb playing? The secret is to strike a black key by using the soft knuckle of the thumb, not the side of the fingernail. That may seem like a small difference but it can revolutionize your technique and, as a byproduct, it will strengthen your 4th and 5th fingers too. I have written many exercises to help you get there.

Feeling comfortable with using your thumb on the black keys will also open the door to landing comfortably after moving large distances across the keys. You may think that speed depends on how fast your fingers can move but it also depends on how quickly you can move your entire arm (and hand) over to the next position on the keyboard.

Challenge #3: Thinking Away "To"

The secret to swiftly and securely moving about the piano is to think away "to" and visualize the thumb and arm pulling your hand laterally across the keyboard to the next destination. If that sounds too abstract, don't worry, there are dozens of exercises here on the Zen of moving away "to."

Zen, schmen…how can you instantly teleport your hand around the keyboard?

It's not that hard to do, especially if you learn to land gracefully way in on the soft pad of that knuckle that we mentioned above. To accomplish this, just have your index or middle finger lightly touch (or nearly touch) the wood on the backboard…this will pull the thumb in and bring the rest of your hand in over all the keys too. This is a fantastic aid when you're improvising music faster than you can think up fingerings! It will also give more accuracy on the white keys too. This move can be compared to an outfielder in major league baseball running to get under a fly ball: their real genius lies in simply getting to where the ball will land…then just holding up their hand to catch it!

THINKING AHEAD, ZEN STYLE

Below is a little Zen-like experiment on which to give this concept a try. It's a simple G scale where, in figure b) below, the scale splits apart. On your first attempt, you will probably be fixated on the first three notes, ie: you will have a sensation that the opening notes G, A and B are "home" or a center of gravity. When the scale suddenly jumps an octave you'll have a sense that the high notes are "far away," that the jump from the low B to high C is difficult or even a bit absurd, especially as you have to cross the thumb under the B to ever have a chance of hitting the high C. Just jump in cold and try playing Fig. b) below a few times and see how you do.

Figure a)   Figure b)

4

Any difficulty you may have had making the jump was probably caused by trying to negotiate the octave leap by using the conventional thumb-under approach.

Now, let's look at another way of thinking about the problem. Mentally erase the lowest three notes that started fig. b) above. Are you done erasing? Good.

Step One - now practice just the notes in fig. a) below. Make it your new home, your center of gravity. For you, no other notes exist. There is the black key F# to play, so keep the hand way in over the keys, thumb over the knuckle on C.

Figure a)

Step Two - OK, if you're totally down with these notes, go ahead and add the missing G, A and B as shown in figure b) below. As you're playing them, *ignore* them. You've already found them, you're on them and in an instant you'll be past them. You need to be focusing your mind on the *second* handful that is up an octave. Don't let the white-key simplicity of the first three notes mess up or pollute the higher, black key, eight-note group that you worked on so hard!

Figure a)   Figure b)

If you were successful in keeping your mind on the high notes even while though you began with the three low notes, then you should have experienced a dramatic improvement in negotiating the octave leap. This is what positional playing is all about: *thinking in handfuls instead of one note at a time*. And the thumb is what leads you there.

> ### *Six Words from Oscar Peterson*
> *Here's a little anecdote to reinforce this idea. When I was a kid I spent time studying with Oscar Peterson at his jazz school in Toronto. He used one phrase a lot: when given an assignment to work up some difficult material, Oscar would always say, "Get your hands over the notes." I always thought was an odd way to put it until many years had passed. Then I realized that part of his physical genius on the piano was that he always intuitively thought ahead to where he was going. It's hard to say whether that came from his awesome, natural technique or because he "heard" fast. It's difficult to separate the two, but in either case that's a great lesson to be learned from him. One of the benefits of mastering the widely spaced pentatonic scales in this book is that they require you to be constantly letting go of wherever you are and thinking "away to." You'll know for sure that you've improved when you can't discern whether your hands have gotten better or your mind has gotten sharper!*

Chapter 2 - Pentatonic Scales: Where in the World Are They From?

The easiest way to visualize a pentatonic scale is to know that it can be played on the five black keys of the piano. If you start out on Eb and end on Db, that will outline the Eb minor version of the scale. There is also a major version, which would run from Gb through Eb. For our purposes we'll begin by dealing mostly with the minor version first.

Both of the scales above have been used in many non-western cultures for centuries. The fact that they have come to play such a vital role in jazz, blues, gospel and hip hop brings up a couple of questions: how did the scales suddenly get established so quickly in Europe and the United States in the late 1800s and why, after a century of common use, can't most pianists finger the pentatonic scales?

EAST MEETS WEST IN BOTH PARIS AND NEW ORLEANS

In the late 1800s, the pentatonic scale was introduced to America and Europe in two widely separated French cities: Paris and New Orleans, Louisiana. Paris was hosting an international world's fair in 1889, *L' Expostion Universell* where, for the first time, Europeans were able to hear improvised music from Asia, Africa and Bali performed. Coincidently, during the very same period in New Orleans, liberal city laws allowed the recently freed slaves to publicly perform African music and tribal rituals in public. Amongst these performances were the very public African funeral ceremonies, which featured marching bands in the streets. All of these were events were strictly forbidden outside the New Orleans city limits in the rest of the Deep South.

SPONTANEOUS MUSIC IN PARIS

At *L' Expostion Universell* (or the "Paris Expo") French Impressionist composers Claude Debussy and Maurice Ravel heard all sorts of non-western musicians improvising with the pentatonic scales on African Marimbas, thumb pianos, Balinese gamelan plus many exotic stringed instruments from Japan. Both composers were so impressed with the simplicity and freedom of these styles that they immediately dumped the use of the complex, intellectually organized and rule-laden forms that had been developed primarily by great German composers like Bach, Mozart and Beethoven. Up to that time, the Germans had been dominating the scene with their philosophy of writing simple, short themes followed by rational, intellectual variations based on them. This inspired a bit of French nationalism, at least on Debussy's part, for he proclaimed that he was "tired of seeing endless German operas where everybody wore a metal helmet and carried a spear!" The irony is that the French had to be inspired by music from 10,000 miles away to find the key to expressing their version of the Gallic soul. The double irony is that America had the same experience in New Orleans: it took music imported from Africa to help the United States find its musical identity too. More about that later.

Here's a way that the pentatonic scale might be played on a Japanese stringed instrument called a *Koto*.

After hearing the simple but powerful spells cast by the pentatonic scale, Debussy and Ravel tried using them to "paint" gentle scenes of water, clouds and fog, thus ridding themselves of the old-fashioned rules and formal musical structures of the Germans. The improvised quality of these Impressionist pieces must have seemed like a pretty radical idea back then because most European ears had been accustomed to hearing music as a series of predictable events, much like what you experience today in a movie or television show. By 1900, the French impressionist composers had gotten rid of distinct musical narratives and were using the newly "discovered" pentatonic scales to portray hazy and ill-defined scenes without much traditional melody or even a sense of beat. They were creating trance pieces that relied on the timbres (sound color) of various instruments to convey moods rather than melodies. Typical titles were "*Nuages*" (Clouds) by Debussy and "*Jeux d' Eau*" (The Play of Water) by Ravel. They were creating sonic paintings before sound movies were ever invented!

Here's an example of how the pentatonic scale might be used by an impressionist composer to simulate waves or ripples in water:

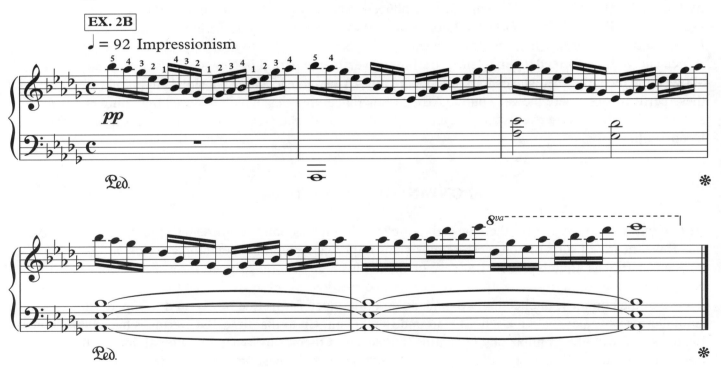

If you were thinking, "Hey, I could do that," you would probably be right. All you have to do is wipe your hand across the black keys and throw in an occasional bass note. You could be completely spontaneous and come up with instant sound-paintings of a vast ocean, water bubbling in a fountain or perhaps even a wild toboggan ride. That's the kind of improvised spontaneity that Debussy and Ravel were trying for.

SPONTANEOUS PAINTINGS IN FRANCE

French impressionist painters Claude Monet and Edgar Degas had also attended *L' Exposition Universelle* where they saw Japanese *sumi* (ink) paintings. These spontaneously created works were quickly brush-painted on delicate scrolls and there was no way to redo anything or make corrections: if you made a mistake you either ruined the painting or ended up poking a hole in the parchment. In a sense, that sounds similar to improvising a jazz solo, right?

The Japanese *sumi* paintings had no central focal point, and with diagonal lines that ran off into nowhere they generally looked like random fragments clipped out of a larger, more important painting. This was visual anarchy by Western standards but the impressionist painters loved them! This ink brush piece certainly doesn't look controversial, except for the fact that it helped inspire radical new art and music in Europe around 1900.

Bamboo - Japanese sumi painting

In a manner similar to what Debussy and Ravel were doing in music, the French painters suddenly abandoned traditional formal lines and started to portray only fragments of a whole or blurry images to convey merely the feeling of a scene. There are no details in this spontaneous Monet panting—your mind is filling them in!

Claude Monet - "Sunrise

These non-centered, slice-of-life forms of the Japanese art and the unfocused images of impressionism could be compared to the pentatonic scale in music which itself has a vague tonal center and simultaneously suggests five different keys at once. Suddenly, music and art were capturing unplanned, fleeting moments in time, which is a perfect definition of improvisation in jazz. Music and art didn't have to concern themselves with great themes and battles or famous people anymore—art might just portray a fragment of bamboo in a spring garden and music might now convey a ripple of water in a manner just as casual as an improvised jazz lick. And this was all going on just as recording technology and emerged to capture these moments in time! Although the directness and simplicity of some of these non-western concepts may seem tame today, they caused quite a stir in both music and art circles by 1900, as did jazz.

Chapter 3 - Music Scandals in America

At exactly the same time, the United States had recently ended slavery (in least in theory) and African-Americans were in the process of developing early blues and gospel styles in the Deep South. Both of these styles sounded about the same except that gospel was about faith and spiritual matters and the blues was about sadness, great joy, irony or simply lamenting the fact that one's baby had just left them. Both of these vocal styles were largely based around the pentatonic scale and were quickly adapted by African-American instrumentalists to be played on European trumpets, trombones, woodwinds and keyboards.

After the Civil war ended in 1865 the newly freed African-Americans formed all sorts of social, religious and self-protective societies or organizations which all sponsored some sort of musical group. During this era a lot of old Civil War surplus military uniforms and marching band instruments had become available in junk stores throughout the south and they were purchased by the various social societies. This formed the basis of their musical groups and usually included a brass marching band, which were all the rage in the late 1800s.

Since African music is largely improvised, it wasn't a stretch for the players to learn to imitate the sounds of vocal blues and gospel on their newly acquired European instruments. This cultural and musical chemistry all mixed in the city of New Orleans. Since it had been owned by the French before the United States purchased it from them 1803, it remained a cosmopolitan, liberal city that allowed African music and even voodoo religious practices to flourish there.

The improvised music in New Orleans that was a product of playing African scales and rhythms on European instruments was not seriously recorded until 1917. The original practitioners considered it a kind of secret club music and thought it might be stolen if recorded. How right they were!

Finally, in 1917, the first commercial jazz recording was released by a group of white musicians who called themselves The Original Dixieland Jazz Band.

The result was explosive! Lots of fear and moral indignation ensued as white America was suddenly exposed to the rhythms and haunting, minor tonalities imported from Africa. The nearly identical pentatonic and six note blues scales had combined with popular dance rhythms and went on to create a 60-year-long period of jazz creativity that lasted into the 1970s.

In the earlier examples 2A and 2B, we saw how a very tranquil vibe could be created in both Japanese music and French impressionism by using the pentatonic scale. Below are two examples of how the scale was transformed by jazz musicians into something quite different: a vehicle for transmitting high energy! Example 2C below is what I call "piano drumming" and 2D is a bit of modern jazz inspired by the jazz master McCoy Tyner.

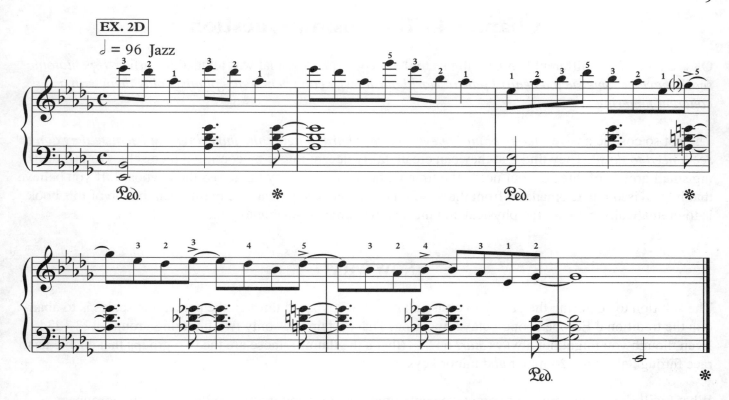

In the previous four examples 2A-B-C-D, we experienced the otherworldliness of a Japanese koto followed by an impressionist waterfall, then a bass and guitar street jam and finally, some urban jazz. We could probably go on all day with even more examples such as children's songs, Irish music, gospel, cowboy songs and soul singing too, but I think the point has been made: the pentatonic scales have a long and varied history and have come to dominate American music over the past 100 years.

Summing Up

In the late 1800s, both America and Europe were suddenly exposed to the pentatonic scale, and then some of the best musical minds of the era proceeded to create and develop new ways of speaking music with it. It's fascinating that all the music influenced by non-Western scales and rhythm seemed to cause so much controversy. Dreamy and ethereal imprtessionist music caused European listeners to wonder if beat and rhythm had disappeared from modern music. And jazz caused the American public to be concerned that too much rhythm would cause moral decay!

Chapter 4 - The Cosmic Question

OK, so all of these different genres bring us to the second question that was alluded to earlier: *If pentatonic scales have become such a central part of world music, why can't very many pianists play them with a coherent fingering?*

The not so cosmic answer: *many pianists never try very hard to figure the fingerings out because they don't see a need to do so.* They find that they can create fairly decent music by confining themselves to just utilizing small groups of three or four notes at a time without straying very far across the keyboard. If you believe that improvised music emanates from the wisdom of the hand as well as the brain, then the job of this book is to dramatically increase the physical and musical resources available to you.

NOW WHAT?

The solution to acquiring the ability to cruise all over the keyboard through the pentatonic scales is to abandon the traditional European one-octave fingering. That system uses only two fingering groups: 123 1234. Even though you might not always *start* on "1" (that's the thumb), those are the two groups that enable us to race through all of the 24 major and minor keys.

What I will show you here is a two-octave pentatonic fingering and it will use *three* fingering groups.

Playing the pentatonic scale through two full octaves involves eleven notes, right? Therefore the right hand fingering for all the pentatonic scales will be some variation of one of the three following patterns:

> A) **1234 124 1245**
> B) **123 1234 1245**
> C) **1234 1234 123**

In Chapter 5 you'll learn the six scales that use the fingering from line A) above. We begin with the Eb minor, "black key" minor pentatonic because that one is actually easier to play than the white-key scales built on A D and E. If you think about it, those three white-key pentatonics contain a total of 15 notes that have to be played on only 7 white keys. Confusion reigns and traffic jams erupt! The solution—practice with your eyes closed. More later on this subject.

Part II: The Minor Pentatonics

This section presents the twelve minor pentatonic scales with special instructions on positioning the hand and an accompanying etude for each one.

Chapter 5 - The Eb Minor, "Black Key" Pentatonic

As you begin to read through all the scales, you should always practice them hands separately. In fact, if you consider yourself to be a "one handed" piano player, you might skip the left hand exercises entirely. That's not recommended though, because the byproduct of involving yourself with two hands is that your playing will benefit in ways that you can't foresee. A central theme in this book is that the hands feed the brain as much as the other way around. Think of how athletic ability or lack thereof shaped the styles of jazz greats such as Charlie Parker and Art Tatum versus Bill Evans, Paul Desmond or John Lewis. And also consider the special case of Ahmad Jamal who had great hands but rarely played fast!

Eb MINOR PENTATONIC

We begin with the Eb minor scale because it's a fingering template for six out of the twelve minor pentatonics.

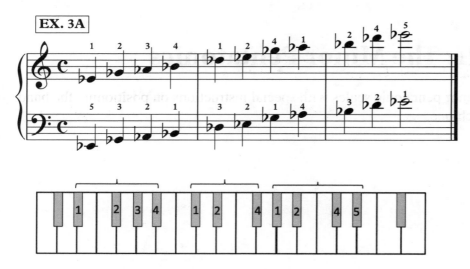

The keyboard diagram above shows how the Eb minor scale divides into three separate fingering-groups or "handfuls" of notes. Each group is indicated with a bracket and requires you to make a new hand shape.

These fistfuls of notes (as shown in Ex. 3B) will place the hand directly over several keys at once and avoid you having to make micro-adjustments at the last instant. Realize that as you play each chord, you've just played the notes infinitely fast. Later you can just slow them down when you play the scale…ha!

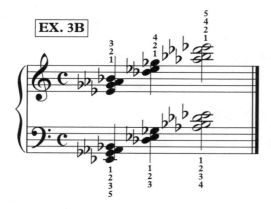

Each fingering group above is physically defined by where the thumb lands. As you practice, use the thumbs as guides to pull each hand to its "target." Be sure to land on the soft knuckle of the thumb and not the side of the nail or it might just slip off the black key! This concept is even more important on the white keys: if your thumb isn't way in on the knuckle and pointing straight ahead, it tends to "X the note" and hit two keys at once. Totally embarrassing!

THINKING AWAY "TO"

Now we're ready to play the scale one note at a time. The challenge is to jump cleanly to each new hand position. To accomplish this, you need to *practice the second fingering group first*. This way you can work up perfect fingering and hand positions for the high notes first without getting them corrupted by anything you may have played a millisecond earlier on a lower part of the keyboard.

To this end, examples 4A-B begin with the second fingering group of the Eb minor scale. Keep the thumb in on the knuckle and the index finger almost touching the backboard. Practice hands separately.

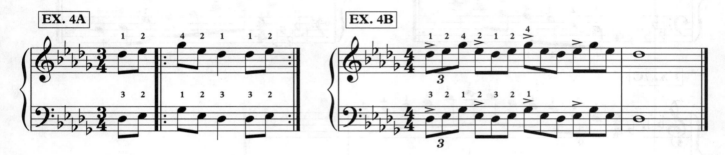

The next step is to add the beginning four notes of the scale to what you just practiced. No turning the thumb under allowed: just "ignore" the first four notes as you play them in Ex. 5A below and already be thinking away "to" the next thumb position. The same idea will rule in 5B: even though the thumb is the last note of this measure, its position will retroactively affect the previous three notes...don't have it dangling over your lap.

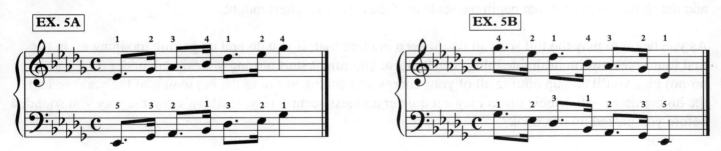

Pretty easy, right? It will be if you're always thinking *away* from your current position and *ahead* to wherever you want to travel to.

In Example #6 on the following page, we'll complete the scale by practicing the highest four-note group. Keep those thumbs way in over the knuckles (you don't want those thumbnails clicking on the keys!).

EX. 6

Now let's add the three notes from the middle group and lengthen the chain.

EX. 7A   **EX. 7B**

EX. 7C

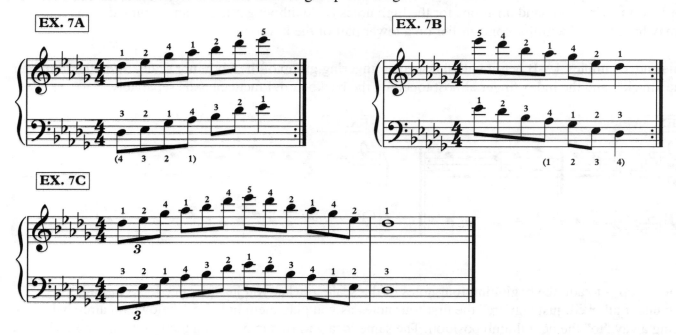

When you're ready to try the complete two-octave scale, you have to keep visualizing the two hand positions you just played in exercises #7 A,B,C above. Just keep living "up there" in your mind and merely add the initial four notes that begin the scale as if they were an afterthought.

As you begin to play the full scale in Ex. 8, keep in mind that, if you do end up getting too hung up in the first four notes, two undesirable things can happen: you might start turning your thumb under (that's a no-no) plus you'll end up putting all of your energy and confidence in to the beginning of the scale and all the higher notes will dribble off as they get quieter and less secure. Hey wait! Isn't that the way you sounded before you picked up this book?

EX. 8

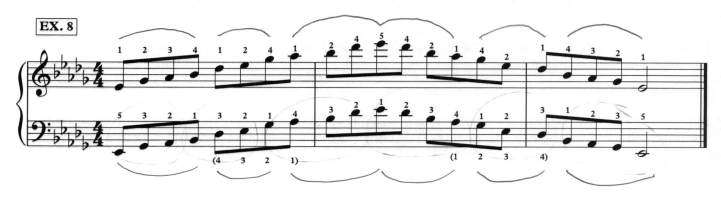

You'll notice that Ex. 8 has an alternate left-hand fingering in parenthesis too. Although this one might feel more natural when playing the left hand by itself, the original fingering above the notes allows both hands to change position simultaneously—much better when improvising!

ETUDE #1 in Eb MINOR

Here's a short etude for the right hand. It should be played with a loping swing feel approximating 12/8 time. It should also be eventually transposed and learned in the all-white, minor keys of A, D and E.

Dr. McCoy, I Presume

NOTE: this simple etude opens the door to a profound concept that will influence your creativity and also how you think about moving around the keyboard. That concept is: *The 5-note pentatonic scale excludes seven out of the twelve notes in an octave. This results in so few notes being left over that the hand has to be constantly hopping to new positions on the keyboard, even if you never skip a scale tone. The physicality of this hopping about is a large part of the creativity.*

What this means is that, when you get bored noodling away at three or four notes under your hand and feel you are ready to move on, the thumb (and arm) will have to do all the moving for you. If you merely let a finger lead you instead of grabbing an entire new handful, you'll probably be OK for an instant but then find that you've suddenly run out of fingers, your thumb is hanging out over your lap and you're generally lost. Sounds like a recipe for disaster, right? And it can all happen in about one second!

Speed Demons
There will be a series of short exercises scattered throughout the book called "Speed Demons." They're mostly for fun, but also to see how fast you can play in whatever key is being covered at that moment. Including an alternate, triplet version helps to avoid the lumpy playing that results from each new hand position starting with the thumb.

Speed Demon #1

The Eb minor scale also works well over Ab7 and Cb major 7th chords.

Chapter 6 - The "White Key" Minor Pentatonics

Now that you've experienced a bit of playing on the black keys, we'll move on to the all-white key pentatonic scales, which will be A, D and E minors. They will use the same fingering as Eb minor and this is where your work with the thumb will really pay off.

A MINOR PENTATONIC

EX. 9A A minor pentatonic

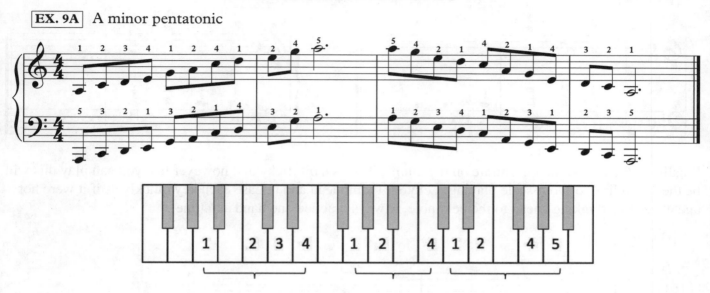

Not as easy as you thought, right? The problem, of course, is all those acres of undifferentiated white keys.

The solution is to practice with your eyes closed. Huh? That's right. That will vastly improve your muscle memory. Many of the greatest musicians ever are blind: Art Tatum, George Shearing, Ray Charles, Lennie Tristano, Stevie Wonder and don't forget Keith Jarrett, Bill Evans and many others who don't look at the keyboard much either!

Ex. 9B, C, and D block the three A minor pentatonic hand positions.

EX. 9B

EX. 9C

EX. 9D

BLOCKING EXERCISES

Now you're ready to practice locating the notes that will transport you to each new position. They will be played by the thumb while traveling up and the 4th finger when coming back down, as shown in Ex. 10A. Ex.10B raises the ante by using two notes. When you remove all of the in-between notes, as we have done here, you can see how fast your entire arm has to jump to get you to the next hand position!

Finally, in Ex.10c we'll concentrate on the thumb. This is a bit tricky and however fast you can play this will be the speed limit of your scale playing. Let your thumb lead and release each key quickly as if it were hot and always be thinking ahead to the next note. Always practice one hand at a time.

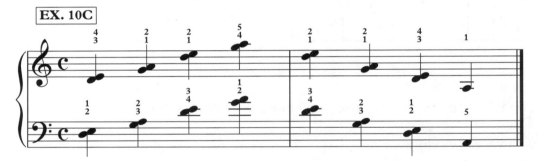

Here's the full scale with dotted rhythms to simulate a jazz swing feeling.

ETUDE #2 in A MINOR

As you play Etude 2, you will see find most of the little groups of notes emanate from the hand positions you just practiced. This occasionally results in an odd fingering situation, as happens in measure 4 where the second finger is used twice in a row. That's because measure 5 moves lower to the "D" hand position.

If you, as an improviser, had played that last note (E) in measure four with the *thumb*, measure five would have certainly ended up being completely different notes!

"A" So Low

Etude Nº2 A minor

Ped. * Ped. *

5
rit.

Ped. * Ped. * Ped. *

Speed Demon #2

The A minor scale also works well over D7 and F major 7th chords.

Nº2

D MINOR PENTATONIC

EX. 12 D minor

BLOCKING OUT D MINOR

Ex. 13A locates the first note in each fingering group and 13B locates the last. 13C then combines the two. Traveling two octaves this fast is the challenge.

ETUDE #3 in D MINOR

Although the tempo marking is fast, this etude can be played at any speed. If you transpose it up a half step, the right hand is all on the black keys.

Night Hawks

(continued on following page)

5

Speed Demon #3
The D minor scale also works well over G7 and Bb major 7th.

Nº3

E MINOR PENTATONIC

EX. 15A E minor

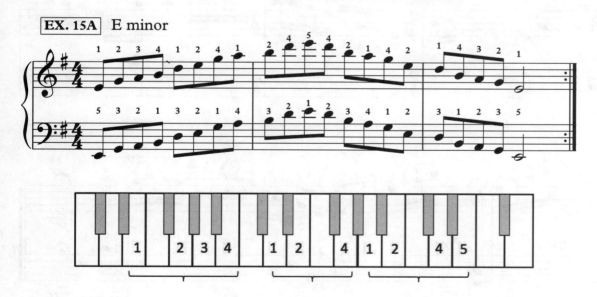

BLOCKING OUT E MINOR

On the next page is a traveling exercise for E minor. If the previous white key scales on A and D haven't prepared you enough yet, then you might want to transpose the D minor exercises (13a, b and c) up a step to E minor.

If you get lost in the snow of white keys, then you should practice the A D and E scales with your eyes closed. Remember the blind pianists like Art Tatum and George Shearing that were mentioned earlier: they never had problems with finding white keys because their hands had more knowledge than our eyes do! Here are the three hand positions for E minor as taken from the keyboard diagram above.

ETUDE #4 in E MINOR

Even though the hand travels quite a bit in this slow piece, most of the notes occur in little four note hand-fuls. The right hand is based on the E minor scale but the left hand chords seem to drift between the keys of C and A major. Mentally add six flats and Etude #4 will automatically be transposed to Eb minor. It sounds great in that key!

Speed Demon #4
The E minor scale also works well over A7 and C major 7th chords.

Chapter 7 - "Single Black Key" Minor Pentatonics

G AND B MINOR SCALES

We now leave the white key scales and enter a new geography of the keyboard. We'll be working with G minor and B minor, both of which contain a single black key.

EX. 16 G minor

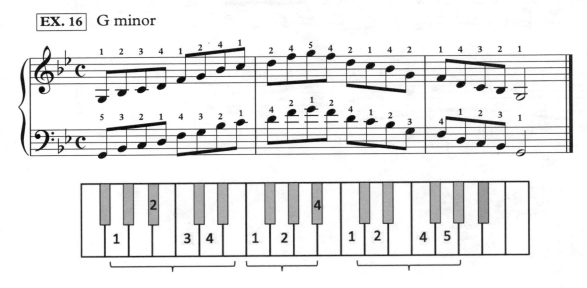

In Ex.16, you can see that the right hand fingering for G minor is the same used in the previous keys, but the left hand is now different. This is to avoid using the thumb on the black key, Bb.

In keeping with our "thinking away to" philosophy, we'll start by practicing the second position notes first. This is the fingering group **1, 2, 4** from the keyboard diagram above. Watch out for the final note, C. There is a sudden jump of the thumb to get you there in place for the third position.

EX. 17A

Ex. 17B has the third position notes. Watch out for the Bb at the end, it prepares you to descend to the second position.

EX. 17B

Now return to Ex. 16 and play the entire the right hand scale.

THE LEFT HAND

We'll start with the second position notes for the left hand. Be prepared for the last note, D. Try not to cross over the top of the thumb to get there: just jump. If you can do that and keep the hand fairly open, you will be over the notes for the third position.

Here are the third position notes. Watch out for the final note C. It prepares you to descend to the second position.

Now go back to Ex. 16 and play the entire two-octave scale with the left hand. Then try playing both hands together.

ETUDE #5 in G MINOR

Circle the all right hand notes in Etude #5 that are played with the thumb. That small task will speed the learning process up tremendously.

Far and Away

Speed Demon #5
The G minor scale also works well over C7 and Eb major 7th chords.

Keeping the hands well in over the keys enables the entire hand to have easy access to the black keys. Back in the era of Bach, the thumb was rarely used at all!

B MINOR PENTATONIC

In Ex.18 below, you see that the right hand uses the same fingering as in the previous keys. The left hand has now changed to avoid using the thumb on F#.

EX. 18 B minor scale

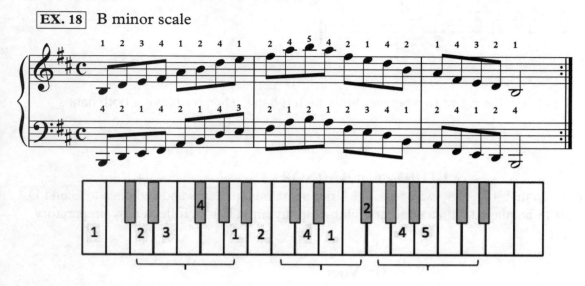

Ex. 19A is mostly for the location of the thumb. In the second measure, you will see that, unless you allow the thumb (usually on the lowest key on each beat) to guide you to each new position, it's difficult to make the hand move very fast.

EX. 19A

Ex. 19B brackets the outer notes of each right hand position. This really gives a sense of how far and fast the pentatonic scales force the entire arm to move.

EX. 19B

THE LEFT HAND

Ex. 19C is for the location of the thumb. As you play the downbeat of the second measure, you have to flip the second finger over the thumb to play the highest note, B. As you reach over for that B, have the thumb maintain its position on the A because you'll be playing it again an instant later.

EX. 19C

Ex. 19D brackets the outer notes of each left hand position.

Now go back to Ex. 18 and play the entire two octaves with the left hand. Then try playing both hands together.

ETUDE #6 in B MINOR

Etude #6 is a bit different in that it breaks away from the strict pentatonic patterns and switches to G and D minors near the end. It is to be played with a straight-eighth note rhythm. (This is followed by preparatory exercises 20-27.)

Sotto Voce

(continued on following page)

Prep exercises for Etude #6

I hope that you found that Etude #6 pretty much played itself. If not, here are a couple of small spots you might want to check out. The challenge here is that they involve the white keys and it's easy to get lost. (Don't forget to practice with your eyes closed.) Exercises 20-25 below will concentrate on the wide intervals found in measures 27 and 28 at the end of the etude.

Ex. 20 is from the second beat of measure 27 as this is where you will want the hand to "live" for a couple of beats.

EX. 20 Etude N° 6 exercises

In Ex. 21 we tunnel backwards to the first beat of measure 27 and merely add two lower notes to the chain. Keep the hand centered as in Ex. 20 above.

EX. 21

Ex. 22 is from the fourth beat of measure 27 and prepares us for measure 28.

EX. 22

Now we transition into measure 28. The little challenge here is that there are two consecutive C's played, each requiring a different finger. Plant your thumb with the knuckle way in over G and then work the upper notes.

EX. 23

Now for the payoff—here are the final two beats of Meas. 27 connected to the first two beats of Meas. 28.

EX. 24

And finally, we're ready to try the entire sequence running from the beginning of measure 27 into 28. You need to rotate your hand slightly clockwise in the second measure so you can tuck your thumb in to play the final note "E."

EX. 25 Measure 27 from Etude N° 6

Exercises 26 A B and 27 below will focus on the seemingly complex passage found in measures 24-25 of the etude. On examination, you can see it's really just arpeggio patterns made from the four simple chord shapes shown in Ex. 26B.

Ex. 26A first locates the thumb notes and then 26B blocks out the "secret" chord shapes.

EX. 26A From measures 24 / 25 of Etude N° 6   **EX. 26B**

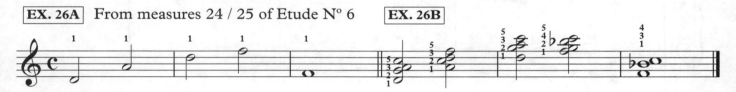

Ex 27 now plays through the notes from the five chords above, one at a time.

EX. 27 Prep for Etude N° 6

Now return to Etude #6 and have some effortless fun. Good luck!

Speed Demon #6
The B minor scale also works well over E7 and G major 7th chords.

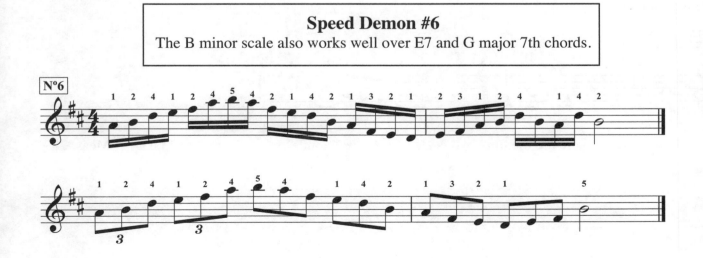

Chapter 8 - C, F and Bb Minor Pentatonics

C MINOR PENTATONIC

C minor has an interesting fingering in the right hand. The ascending fingering is the usual mixed bag of stuff that changes every octave but the descending pattern clones itself out every five notes:
(5) 42131 42131, etc.

Some people take the descending fingering used here and reverse it, using it to go up the C minor scale. It's an easy and strong fingering if you're only going up one octave, but for larger ranges it's a bit clumsy.

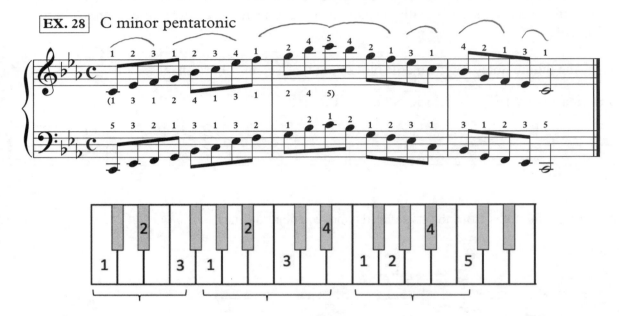

Since C minor involves two black keys, here are two ascending exercises with a different approach. Ex.29A emphasizes the top note of the first two hand positions or, where you are traveling "to." Keep the weight away from the thumb and toward the 3rd and 4th fingers playing the half-notes. The bottom notes are to be released quickly.

Ex. 29B transports you from the second position up to the third position. Again, emphasize the top notes and quickly release the bottom ones, as if the key is too hot to touch!

EX. 29B

Then proceed to 29C when you're ready.

EX. 29C

In Ex. 30 we train the thumb to lead us down the scale. Pianists are accustomed to bringing out the highest note, so concentrating on the low notes with thumb may seem a bit counterintuitive.

EX. 30

Here's a final two-octave walkthrough with the thumb.

EX. 31A

Here's a velocity study. It's kind of amazing how fast you can play this flurry of 24 notes when you know where to throw the hand!

EX. 31B

ETUDE #7 in C MINOR
(This etude is followed by preparatory exercise 32.)

Sparrow's Point

Etude #7 Prep exercise

Ex. 32 opens up the hand for the octave-wide span of notes at the beginning of Etude #7. Even though the thumb may seem to be about last thing a player might be concerned with here, it's what holds it all together. There are several places in this etude where the thumb transports the hand to the first note in each new register.

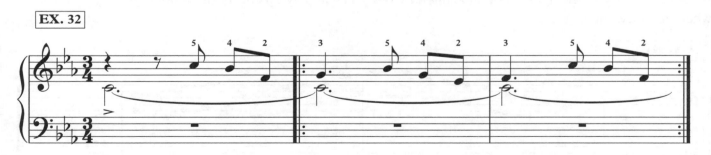

F MINOR PENTATONIC

The bad news is that F minor scale has three black keys and we finally cannot avoid using the thumb to play one of them in the right hand. The good news is that the descending fingering is a easy repeating pattern: **(5)31 321 31 321,** etc.

Why not use the descending fingering while traveling up? No reason—except that, if speed is what you need, it's not very fast.

EX. 33 F minor pentatonic

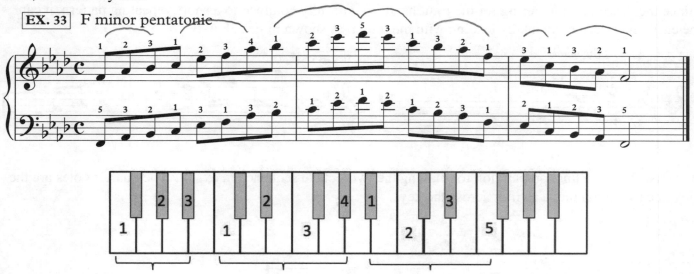

Ex. 34A transports you from the first position up through the second. Notice that the upper notes go up by fourths. Keep the weight on them and release bottom notes quickly.

EX. 34A

36

Ex 34B deals with that pesky B that the thumb has to play in measure two. It's easy if you slide the hand way in to the backboard of the piano. In other words, touch the wood with your knuckles and the thumb will be dragged into perfect position over Bb. When you're ready, proceed to Ex. 34C.

Ex. 34D is a thumb placement exercise for the left hand: it plays 7 out of the 20 notes involved in running up and down the two octave F minor scale (in case you weren't counting.)

Since the descending fingering for the right hand is mercifully confined to a short, repeating pattern, it can be easily mastered by mentally leading with the thumb as shown in Ex. 35 A-B.

Exercise 36 is the final preparation for playing the two-octave sequence in ex. 37. The quarter notes are the downbeats, which move swiftly across the keys.

ETUDE #8 in F MINOR

Out of the Blue

Speed Demon #8
The F minor scale also works well over Bb7 and Db major 7th chords.

Bb MINOR PENTATONIC

Good news! Bb minor contains 4 black keys and only one white one. That means that the hand doesn't have to alternate as much between the peaks and valleys of the keyboard.

EX. 38   Bb minor pentatonic

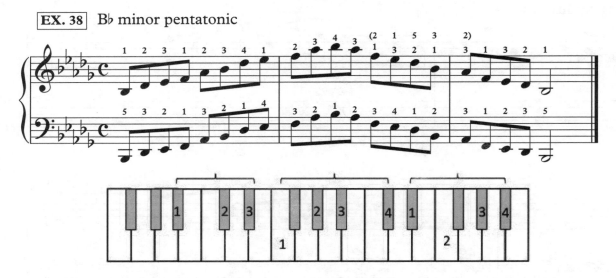

Ex. 40 is the entire two-octave thumb sequence. The descending portion sends the hand down the keys at a fast pace, so don't let the white key F's fool you into pulling away from the backboard.

EX. 40

Ex. 41 is the final positioning exercise prepares you for the first note of each triplet in Ex. 42.

EX. 41

EX. 42

ETUDE #9 in Bb MINOR

Etude #9 is based on little blocks of notes based around specific hand positions. As we've stressed many times, your thumb is the locator of those positions. So even though the thumb may occur near the end of phrases here, it's still helpful to locate its position *first*, to secure an uninterrupted flow of the hand. The left hand is about 80% of what this piece is about—learn it first.

Prep exercises 42 A and B both block out the first two measures of Etude #9, each in a slightly different way. Note that on the third beat of both examples, the thumb is on the high note F and the 3rd finger is on the lower note Eb.

L.A. Uncovered

(continued on following page)

Speed Demon #9

The Bb minor scale also works well over Eb7 and Gb major 7th chords.

Chapter 9 - C#, F# and Ab Minor Pentatonic

C# MINOR PENTATONIC

C# minor is fairly easy to play because of the symmetrical fingering going both up and down. The only tricky part is getting the thumb over the G# that begins the second measure.

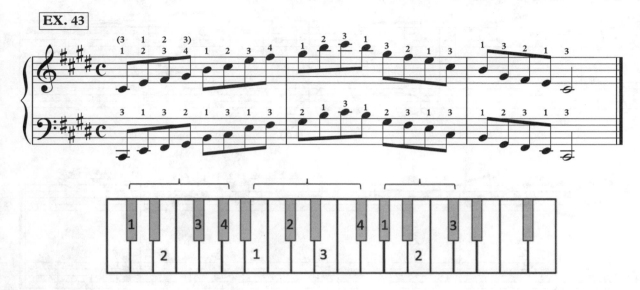

In Ex. 44A, when you go for that G# in the second measure, land on it with your thumb way in over the key.

Watch out for couple of hidden tricks in the first measure of Exercise 44B:

1) The thumb plays the top note B on the second beat of measure #1. But one beat earlier, B is played by the *index* finger.

2) On the same first and second beats, the third finger has to inconvenience itself by jumping from C# down to G#.

ETUDE #10A in C# MINOR

This is Etude 7, originally in C minor, transposed up a half step.

Sparrow's Point II

ETUDE #10B in C# MINOR

(This etude is followed by four prep exercises: #45 A, B, C and 46.)

Imaginary Places

(continued on following page)

Preparatory exercises for Etude #10B

Ex. 45A is a blocking exercise for the first three measures of Etude 10B above. Hold the thumb loosely down on B and rotate the rest of the hand slightly to the right as needed.

EX. 45A

44

Ex. 45B walks you through measures 3 and 4. The note B is the key to mastering this one. It occurs three times with a different finger playing it each time.

Ex. 45C cover measures 7 and 8. It sounds like a miniature chorale.

Ex. 46 takes you from the last beat of measure 10 through 11. Concentrate on getting that 5th finger in the right hand to move about and this should be easy.

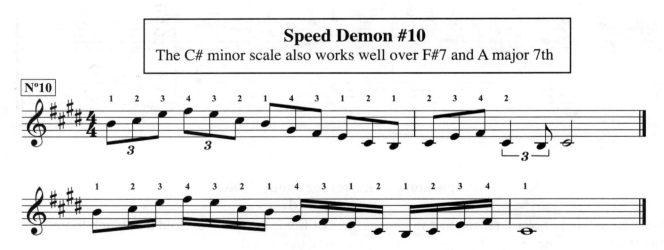

Speed Demon #10
The C# minor scale also works well over F#7 and A major 7th

F# MINOR PENTATONIC

The right hand uses the same fingering as the C# pentatonic. The left hand is a bit easier because there are only two black keys. The keyboard diagram below Ex. 47 contains a third alternate fingering for your consideration.

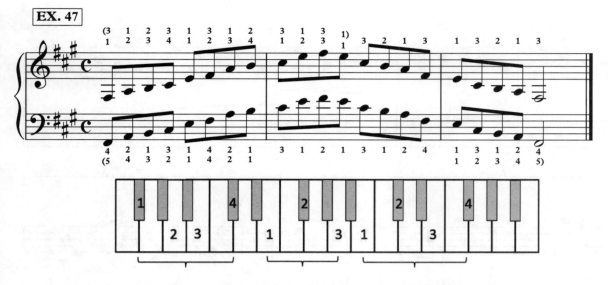

EX. 47

ETUDE #11A in F# MINOR

This etude carries the melody in the left hand. The busy right hand is actually the accompaniment and should fade into the background. Think of an acoustic guitar playing the right hand notes and the left hand as being a cello or tenor saxophone. (This etude is followed by prep exercises #48A B)

Etude N°11A

Olympic Rain Shadow

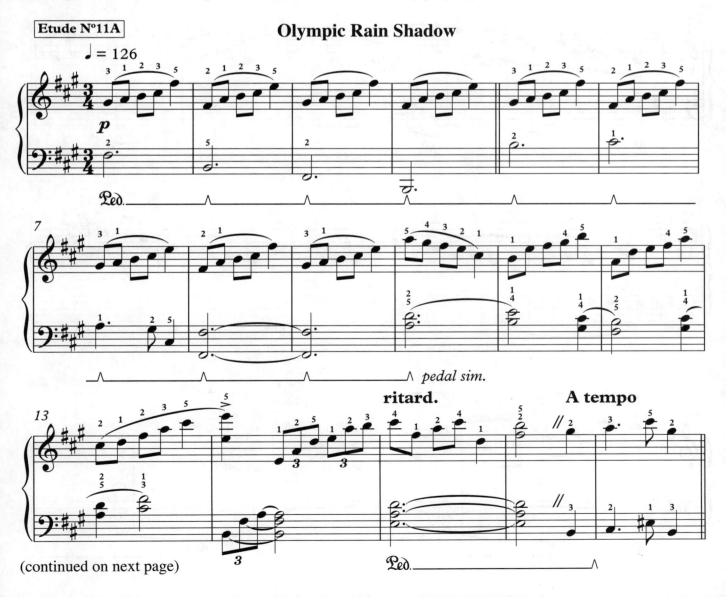

(continued on next page)

46

Prep exercises for Etude #11A

48A blocks out the first nine measures. Once again, he thumb again unifies all the notes in these measures… just keep it tucked in over the A, it's not going anywhere for a while!

Ex. 48B walks you through measures 11-13 where you have to pick up the entire hand several times. Try practicing just the top notes by themselves too.

ETUDE #11B in F# MINOR

(This etude is followed by prep exercises 49 and 50)

Farm Road 602

(continued on following page)

Prep exercises for Etude #11B

Ex. 49A defines both the rhythm articulation and hand positions in measures 1-3. The notes in measure 2 should sound dry and crisp, like a snapping twig…and the upbeats are held back so they enter on the third triplet.

EX. 49A

Ex. 49B is about the sudden changes in volume in measures two and three. Everything is played quietly except for the *sfz* and *ff* markings.

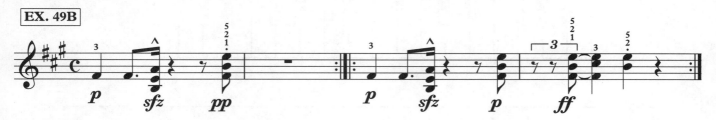

Ex. 49C puts it all together in measures 1-4 with dynamics, articulations and four different hand positions. Exaggerate the dynamics so everything is either very soft or loud.

Ex. 50A starts at the end of measure 8 and goes through measure 12. It highlights the downbeats as the hand crab walks to the left over a space of two octaves.

Now we crab walk two notes at a time. This may seem unorthodox but when you run through meas. 8-12 in the etude, the notes will almost play themselves! It's all about just getting the hand over the notes.

Ab MINOR PENTATONIC

The Ab minor scale is one of the easier ones to play. Both hands change position at the same time and the fingerings occur mostly in four-note groups, which simplifies things a bit.

(continued on following page)

50

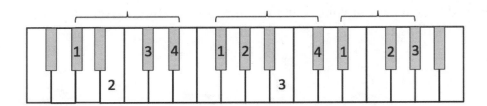

Examples 52 ABCD all demonstrate a good way to practice this subtle shifting of the weight back and forth. The half notes are the keys on which you center the weight of the hand, however lightly or briefly that may be. The quarter notes are a light staccato.

Ex. 52A blocks out the first position of the A minor pentatonic plus the jump over to the second. You should practice just the half notes to sense the weight alternating from the left side of the hand over to the right side, ie: the thumb to the 4th finger and back again.

EX. 52A

Ex. 52B blocks out the second position plus the jump over to the third. Note that Gb appears in both measures 2 and 3. On the first Gb, you have to center the hand's weight on the 3rd finger (on the Ab). In measure 3, you have to immediately transfer the weight over to the thumb (on Eb). In neither case does Gb get much weight. If in doubt, just practice the half notes by themselves a few times.

EX. 52B

Ex. 52C blocks out the whole scale over two octaves. However fast your hand can play this will be the limit of your scale speed.

Ex. 52D blocks out the descending hand positions for the lower half of the two octave scale. Be aware that the half-notes are rapidly moving down the keyboard by perfect fourths.

ETUDE #12 in Ab MINOR

This is pretty much a basic, position-oriented piece. In fact, it's merely a slightly altered version of the A minor Etude #2 from Chapter four.

5th Ave. and East 76th

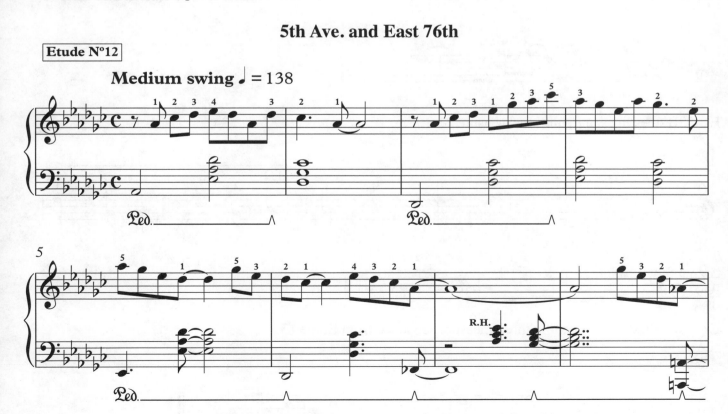

(continued on following page)

ETUDE #13 in Ab MINOR

There are two versions of Etude 13. Version 13A is the easy one and 13B is more challenging. We'll begin with a few details from 13A, which is the shorter version with an easy left hand part.

First, here are some warm ups for the repeated notes that begin the etude.

In Ex. 53A, the half notes are the downbeats found in the first measure of the etude. Lean into these but play the staccato harmony notes very lightly. You can see where your hand will alternately leaning right and left as you walk through the sequence of half-notes Ab, Gb, Gb, Eb and Eb. This prioritizes how the weight will be distributed across the palm when playing the fast repeated notes.

Ex. 53B does the same thing for measures 2-3.

Ex. 53C is the entire opening three-measure sequence from Etude 13.

EX. 53C

OCTAVE BENDING

Ex. 54 A, B and C deal with the thumb slide at the end of measure four. This is what I call *octave bending*. Many players would prefer to simply slide two B flats, an octave apart, up a half step to the C flats. To my ears it sounds way more hip to crush the Bb and Cb together. In order to sound "natural" (like a guitar or voice) the Bb grace note is emphasized and the C flat that follows should be almost inaudible. Keep the hand turned slightly clockwise to allow the thumb to effortlessly grab a big hunk of that Bb.

Here's the thumb slide in context (from measures 4-5 in Etude 13A.)

Exercises 55 ABCD deal with the octave bending found in measure 10. In 55C you need to anticipate the thumb going in over the Db.

Don't rush the thumb slide too much in 55D (on following page). Try slowing the final two notes way down…you might be surprised at how cool that sounds. It simulates the Db decaying and melting into the D like wax dripping down a candle!

EX. 55D

ETUDE #13A in Ab MINOR

Here's the easy version of Etude 13A. The more difficult 13B follows. Be on the lookout for all the C flats, they are in the key signature and they really do exist!

A Bigger Picture

Etude Nº13A

Medium swing ♩ = 120

A Bigger Picture II
(Full version)

Etude Nº13B

Medium swing ♩ = 120

Chapter 10 - Section Review
THE 12 MINOR PENTATONIC FINGERINGS

A minor

D minor

E minor

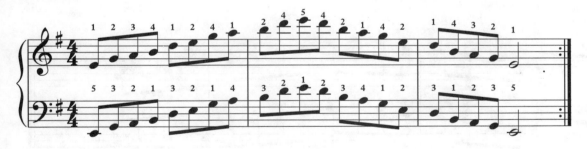

B minor

58

G minor

C minor

F minor

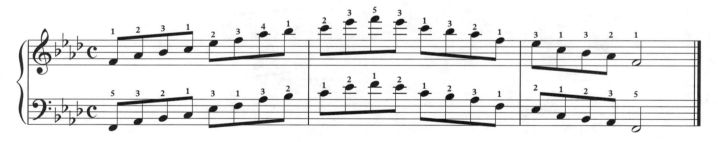

Bb minor

Eb minor

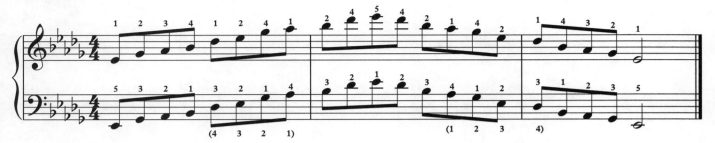

Ab minor

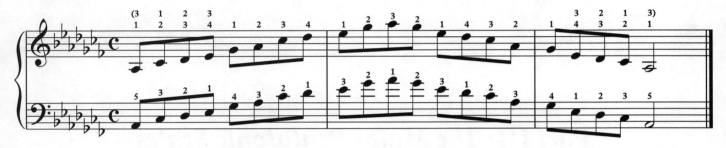

C# minor

F# minor

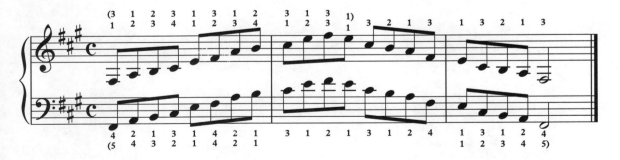

Part III: The Major Pentatonic Scales

A brief introduction to the major pentatonic scale followed by some special effects with which to color them.

Chapter 11 - The Major Pentatonic Scale and Note Bending

So far, we've spent a lot of time on the minor pentatonic scales. They're used frequently because they closely resemble the blues scale and because jazz generally seems to find a lot of use for minor chords and scales. But we now need to meet the *major* pentatonics because they will give you an entirely different handhold and earful on the keyboard. As we'll see in a later chapter of this book, they're more versatile than the minor scales in blending with many different chords and they can provide an exhilarating ride, especially on the white keys.

Earlier, we briefly mentioned that there was both a major and minor version of the pentatonic scale. In the Eb minor example below, you can see that the first four notes collectively outline a minor triad. But in the Gb major version, the first four notes outline a *major* triad. Just understand that a major pentatonic scale uses exactly the same notes as its relative minor (that's the one that starts three half-steps below the major scale.)

C MAJOR PENTATONIC

Ex. 56

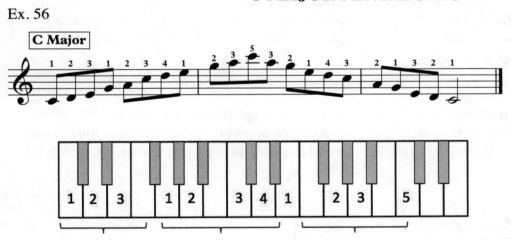

As you can tell, the major pentatonic scale isn't very bluesy and, in it's pure form, went out of fashion in the jazz world in the 1940s. Today it's mostly found in country or hillbilly music and is best used when "painting" pastoral or rural scenes. The composer Aaron Copland, guitarist Pat Metheny and vibraphonist Gary Burton have used this to great effect.

The major pentatonic scales contain no blues notes or minor notes and thus will remain somewhat emotionally neutral until you add some special effects to color them. We'll look at two of these cool effects in this chapter: *bending notes* and *top-harmony*. These will add the fluid quality of a guitar or voice to your piano playing and you'll see that it's quite easy to emote without having to play a million notes. You will also begin to understand that *if you play the major pentatonic scales "dry," the music will die*. Wow, that could make a nice bumper sticker slogan!

We'll delay learning the fingerings for the 12 major pentatonic scales until the end of this chapter after you've become acquainted with note bending and top-harmony. For now we'll confine ourselves to just the C and G scales to test-drive these two special effects a bit.

> **BENDING NOTES**
> **Bending is where you decorate a note by sliding up to it from either one or two half-steps below, just as guitar players do. These are not classical grace notes, so you have to play them with a *decay effect* to avoid sounding like Mozart!**

So, what is the decay effect?

Example 57 demonstrates the decay trick that will lead you to a natural "bent" sound. We'll arbitrarily select an E as an unadorned melody note that we want to bend up "to."
   1) First, start out *loudly* on the D that's two half-steps below.
   2) Next, play the D# with less volume.
   3) Finally, slide very quietly into the destination note E that we're traveling to, using almost no volume at all. Play the fingering as marked and you'll effortlessly achieve that effect of the D and D# "decaying" into the E.

EX. 57

Example 58A has a C major pentatonic lick with no effects to dress it up. This is followed, in 58B, by the more natural sounding of bending the D up to E. The opening grace notes in 58B use the same loud to soft decaying effect as the bent notes leading up to the E. The odd fingering here prepares you for Ex. 58B.

EX. 58A

EX. 58B

Ex. 59 is an extended version of Ex. 58B with the note G added above to get the *top harmony* effect. Ironically, the more complex that the effects are, the more natural the jazz sound becomes. The goal is avoid the dry sound of "typing" on the keyboard and to emulate the flexible pitch of the voice or guitar.

EX. 59

You should now try transposing 58A, 58B and 59 to the keys of F and G.

BENDING TO THE FOURTH

The fourth degree of the scale is another great note to bend, so we'll digress for a moment from the major pentatonic scale back to the minor.

Example 60A is the plain C minor pentatonic idea followed by the "bent" version in 60B. (I like that word "bent"…ha!)

EX. 60A

EX. 60B

The fourth can also be approached from a half step *above*. Example 60C is yet another version of Ex. 60A, except it slides *down* onto the F from F♯ and also adds a bit of top harmony too.

EX. 60C

BENDING TO THE FIFTH

The fifth is probably the most powerful and commonly used note to "cry on" in blues and jazz. For a change of pace, we'll shift to the key of G.

Here is a plain idea built on the G minor pentatonic scale. Learn the rhythm well, otherwise it may get lost when you add all the flowers and feathers in Ex. 61B!

EX. 61A

And here's the full version with top harmony and bent notes flying everywhere. Work this one up and you'll be sounding like Ray Charles or Gene Harris!

EX. 61B

BENDING TO THE SIXTH

Bending up to the sixth is used a lot in country music. But when played against a dominant 7th chord it quickly conveys a deep blues groove. The blandness of the major pentatonic scale can be a bit iffy in a jazz context unless it is tinged with either note bending or funky harmonies, as will be demonstrated in Etude #14.

ETUDE #14

We'll finish and sum up this section on note bending in Etude #14 with a little 12 bar blues that features lots of bending up to the sixth degree of the scale.

Before you get lost in all the slipping and sliding going on in Etude 14, you should first play the simplified version of the first four measures as shown in example 62. It is a slow, rolling, relaxed tempo and the odd fingerings used here are to prepare the hand for dealing with the actual bending effects in the full etude version.

Etude #14 Warmup

Radiator Whiskey

(continued on following page)

Chapter 12 - Meet The Majors

THE 12 MAJOR PENTATONIC FINGERINGS

The first four major scales below all share the same fingering as B major.
All of the twelve scales are arranged according to how they feel to the hand, not by key signature.

Ex. 63

68

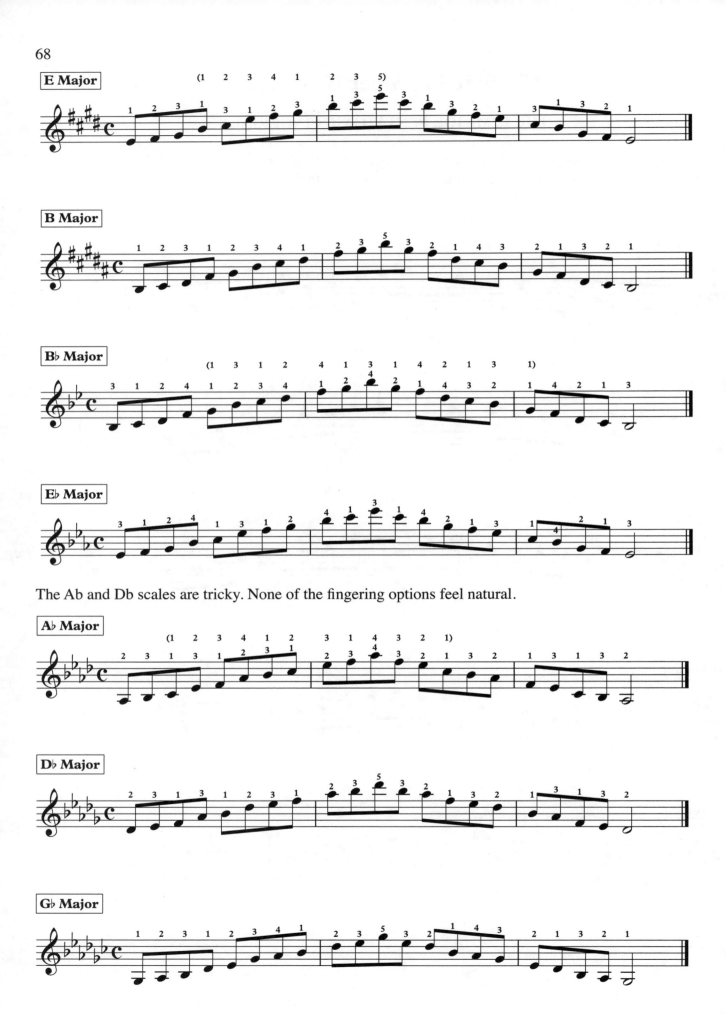

The Ab and Db scales are tricky. None of the fingering options feel natural.

Part IV: The Blues Scale

We'll take a temporary detour from the five-note pentatonic scales to examine the six-tone blues scales.

Chapter 13 - The C and G Blues Scales

(Everyone's Favorite!)

The blues scale is virtually identical to the minor pentatonic scale. It's a difference of just one note: you just add the flatted fifth (or sharp fourth) to the pentatonic scale and *presto*, you've entered a whole new emotional spectrum! A lot of the practice routines and hand jumping covered earlier will apply here and should really pay off big time for you. You may find that some of the mobility you will acquire here will enable you to be able compete with fast and powerful instruments like the guitar and saxophone.

The C Blues Scale

We'll start with the C blues scale because it's familiar to many and has a nice mix of black and white keys. There is an alternate fingering under the notes that is easier to play but does confine you to a one-octave box. Ex. 64A

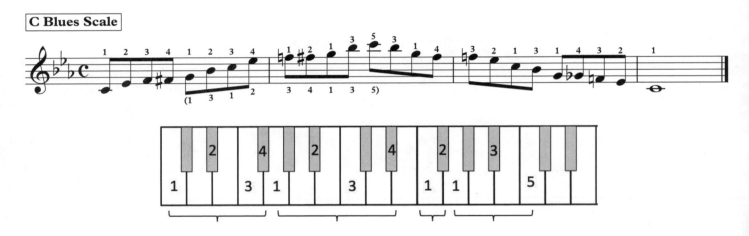

The left hand fingering going up is: **531 4321 31 4321** Coming down: **1234 13 1234 135**

If you find that this scale is a bit of a finger buster, example 64B is a little prep exercise to help ease your pains. I selected just the downbeats from Ex. 64A and they're all C, F or G and played with the just 1st and 3rd fingers. As you play these, they convey no sense of being a blues scale but once you locate them, you can traverse your entire arm across the keyboard as easily as it were suspended by strings.

Here's a triplet version of the C blues scale.

EX. 65A

In Ex. 65A above, all the downbeats are either C or F#. This reveals the real difficulty: only two different note names but with totally unpredictable fingering on each one! The following downbeat exercise should help clear the air.

EX. 65B

The Major vs. Minor Third Quandry

A cool thing about the blues scale is that, even though the 3rd is flatted, you don't have to exclude the major third degree. This part of the scale is flexible in African music and therefore it's flexible and "negotiable" in blues and jazz too. In a major key it sounds good to have the minor third blues note clashing against the major harmony. Conversely, in a minor key it sounds equally good to have the major third of the scale clash against the minor harmony. To some, that's an acquired taste but try it anyway. If incorrectly done it can feel like a piece of tin foil touching a filling, but at least you can get a laugh at a party!

ETUDE #15

Etude 15 on the following page demonstrates how you can bend down to the minor third, even in a minor key (check out measures 2 and 3.) The piece may look intimidating with all those grace notes, so just omit them until a passage swings and then reinsert them as an afterthought.

Lazy Bones

The G Blues Scale

The G blues scale uses the same fingering as C but has only two black keys instead of three. The fingering above the notes is very fast but uses weaker fingers. The fingering below the notes is sturdier but requires more position changes to travel two octaves.

Ex. 66

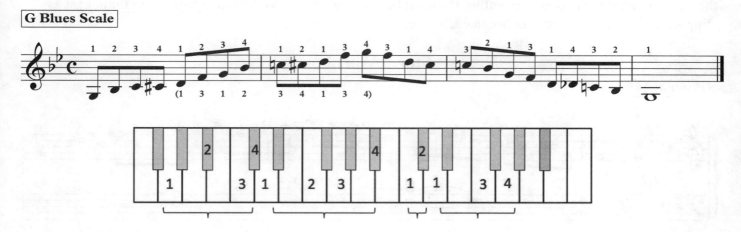

The left hand fingering going up is: **531 4321 31 4321** Coming down: **1234 13 1234 135**

Here's a triplet version of the scale.

EX. 67A

Ex. 67B Blocks out the downbeats for all the triplets in 67A above. Seven of the thirteen notes here are played with the 4th finger!

EX. 67B

ETUDE #16

Lest you be tempted to fall back into old habits by using only the one-octave fingering, Etude 16 begins in the second hand-position of the scale (starting on D instead of the home note G.) The important point here is that starting in the middle of the scale creates different music.

This is a fast, bebop piece that should be played with a light touch. Remember, always think *away to* where the hand is going next. To avoid getting the hand bogged down by playing too legato, try to think of it as slipping a piece of sandpaper between each note.

Storm Warning

Chapter 14 - The F and B Blues Scales

The F and B blues scales both share a simple one-octave fingering. All of a sudden, the key of B doesn't seem so hard any more. What a relief!

The F Blues Scale

Ex. 68

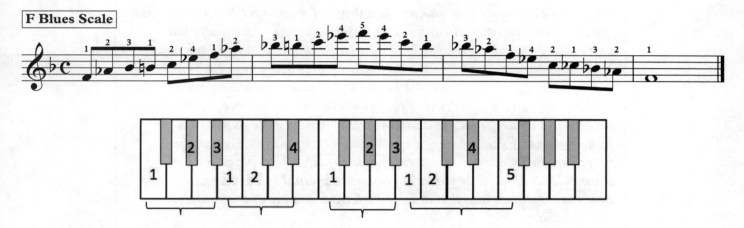

(The left hand fingering going up is: **5321 421 321 421** Coming down: **124 123 124 1235**)

The B Blues Scale

Here is the B blues scale which has odd similarities to the F scale. It has the same 3rd and 7th as an F7 chord and they both share the same blues scale fingering.

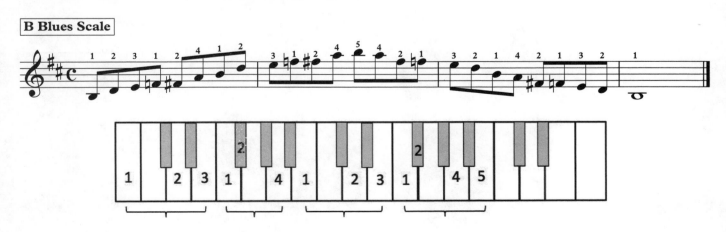

ETUDE #17 and the Floor Drum

Introducing the Floor Drum

Etude #17 in F will require a very particular mindset, otherwise the rhythms and articulations won't make much sense. The key to acquiring this mindset comes from whether you think of a measure in terms of four quarter-notes or two half-notes. The difference may seem subtle but it can make or break a given style. An example might be a fast "two-beat" Dixieland song such as "When the Saints Come Marching In." Ever hear a drummer try to play it in a 4/4 bebop style? It sounds weak and unconvincing, especially if the rest of the band is thinking in "two." Remember, jazz always comes from the dance—in this instance the dance is done to half-notes. It's the same with fast samba rhythms too. By dancing or marching two steps per measure, people are, in effect, playing a floor drum with their feet! If you try to impose a mental reference grid of four beats per measure into this music, it's harder to play and it sounds amateurish.

In Etude #17 on the following page, your "floor drum" will be beating in two (on the 1st and 3rd beats of each measure) so your foot tapping (physical or mental) is crucial. Note that the tempo marking is 72 *half notes* per minute, not 144 *quarter notes*. If you have the half-note establish your floor drum pulse, the listener should perceive that the tempo is approximately one beat per second, even though the right hand notes are moving fast. There are many left hand half-notes in measures 5 through 10 to establish this "slow" beat. The 1/8th-note rhythms are of the legit, straight-eighth variety…no swing allowed here.

Lastly, the best way to find the perfect groove is to base your tempo around all the busy 16th notes occurring in measures 8 through 10. Getting this right may cause the beginning of the piece to sound slow but it will hold together in the end.

Notoriety

Chapter 15 - A, D and E Blues Scales

Blues scales built on A, D and E all use the same fingerings and share the identical geography on the keyboard so if you learn one, you've learned all three.

The A Blues Scale

Ex. 70A

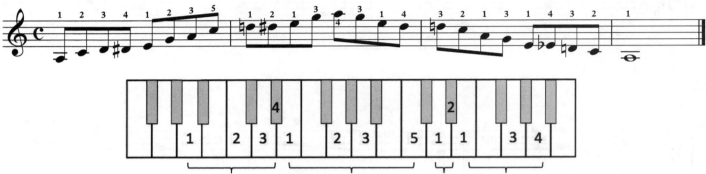

(The left hand fingering going up is: **531 321 421 4321** Descending: **1234 124 123 135**)

The D Blues Scale

Ex. 71A

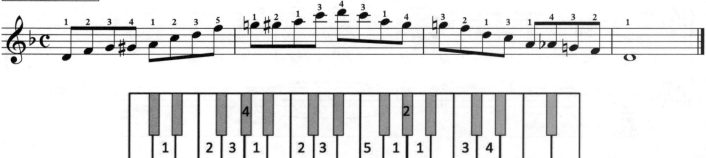

(The left hand fingering going up is: **531 321 421 4321** Coming down: **1234 124 123 135**)

EX. 71B

Escaping Major 7th Hell

In addition to funky environments, the blues scale also works very well with bland, major seventh chords too. (I like to think of it as a soulful way to escape major seventh hell.) Even though the blues scale has an earthy sound that would seem to be the polar opposite of the "prettiness" conveyed by major sevenths, there is a way to blend the two. This blending is based around the simple fact that any major seventh chord is actually a minor triad with a different bass note added below it.

To illustrate this point, an F major 7th chord is actually an A minor triad floating over an F bass note. Therefore the A blues scale you just learned can be used to play over an F major 7th chord.

In Ex. 72A below, the F root is moved down an octave in measure two and you can plainly see that the three notes remaining above spell an A minor chord.

EX. 72A

In the same fashion, the D blues scales from Ex. 71A and B will work with a Bb major 7th chord because it's actually a D minor triad suspended over a Bb bass.

EX. 72B

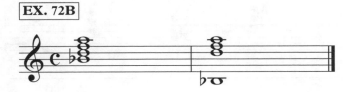

ETUDE #18

Etude #18 will demonstrate how the A, D and F blues scales can be played over totally different bass notes. Before we get to that, Ex. 73 has a simplified version of the first four measures of Etude #18 with the blues scale fragments labeled with their original chord roots in the left hand.

The strange right hand fingering is to prepare the hand for the note bending in the full etude version that follows.

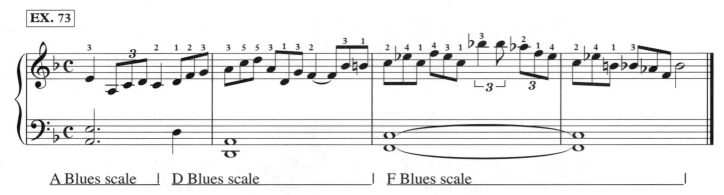

A Blues scale | D Blues scale | F Blues scale |

Etude #18 may now surprise you when you hear how using rich harmonies can transform those A, D and F blues scales into something quite elegant!

Sweet Thing

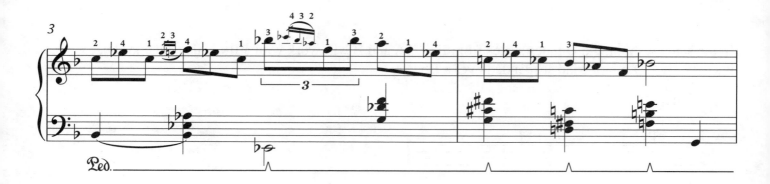

(continued on following page)

The lesson here is that a blues scale doesn't have to be taken at face value, ie: an A blues scale doesn't necessarily have to be played just on an A major or minor chord.

The E Blues Scale

Ex. 74A

(The left hand fingering going up is: **531 321 421 4321**   Coming down: **1234 124 123 135**)

EX. 74B

ETUDE #19

Here's your chance to try the floor drum concept again. This etude is a velocity study to be played as fast as you'd like but your speed will be limited unless you pat your foot in the proper way. If you think of the rhythm as a series of three fast beats per measure, you'll get bogged down. If, on the other hand, you think of each measure as one long beat, you can go like the wind.

The best way to accomplish this is to think of the left hand as the floor drum and the right hand, just supplying some filler. No legato playing in the right hand: visualize inserting a piece of sandpaper between each note, think away "to" and use the pedal lightly to connect things.

Here is a blocking exercise for the first few measures.

EX. 75A

EX. 75B

Ex. 76A and B are from measures 5 and 6. They're a bit of a finger buster because the thumb often plays the highest note!

EX. 76A

EX. 76B

The Floor Drum

Chapter 16 - Bb and Eb Blues Scales

The Bb and Eb blues scales are similar to one another in that they use the same fingerings and are both easy to play. I will be present them here with no comment and we'll move right on to the final three, most difficult blues scales, F#, C# and Ab.

Ex. 77A

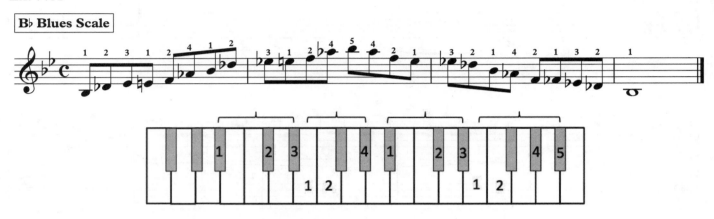

(The left hand fingering going up is: **5321 421 321 421** Coming down: **124 321 124 1235**)

Here is the triplet version of the Bb blues scale with a different key signature. Some people feel more comfortable with fewer accidentals to read.

EX. 77B

Eb Blues Scale

Ex. 78A

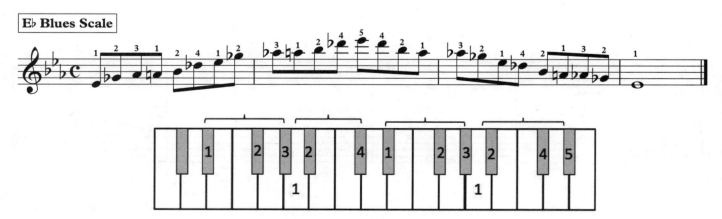

85

(The left hand fingering going up is: **5321 321 321 321** Coming down: **123 123 123 1235**)

EX. 78B

Chapter 17 - Ab, F# and C# Blues Scales

The Ab, F# and C# Blues Scales are the nasty, bad boys of all scales. They start on the 3rd finger instead of the thumb and generally feel pretty awkward. But there are a couple of tricks to help things out a bit. More on those in a minute.

The Ab Blues Scale

Ex.79

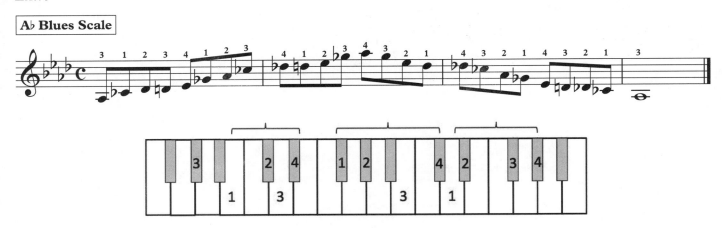

(The left hand fingering going up is: **4321 4321 31 321** Coming down: **123 13 1234 1234**)

Here are some blocking exercises. In Ex. 80A, be aware that the right hand thumb has to make a fast diagonal move all way up from Cb to the Gb so keep the hand turned slightly counter-clockwise until the beginning of the second measure. Also, try skipping the Ab on the first beat. Add it in later after your thumb is comfortable making the Cb to Gb leap.

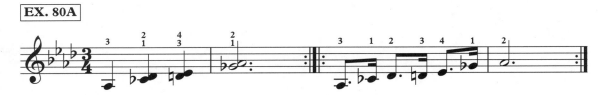

Ex. 80B blocks out the second half of the scale. The hand should be pointed straight ahead for the first two beats and then rotated slightly to the left on the third beat and in measure two.

Now go back and practice the full scale in example 79.

In Ex. 81 we'll switch to an easy, *three-finger* pattern that works naturally with triplets. In this case, the thumb conveniently occurs on each downbeat. **123 124 123 1245**. The descending fingering is: **5421 321 421 321**.

EX. 81

For fresher jazz ideas, a cool trick is to start an idea on any note except for Ab with the thumb. Then limit yourself to only two "handfuls." Examples 82 A and B both use the finger pattern: **1234 12345** and allow you to cover almost two octaves with only one jump! The object here is to try as many different handholds as possible on the difficult scales. Finding certain clusters of notes that feel "friendly" to your hands can make you forget that Ab is a challenging key.

EX. 82A

EX. 82B

Speed Demon #11

Here is a speed demon workout with identical notes in two different rhythm patterns. Example 83A is slightly easier than 83B because the thumb occcurs on the beats. Note that each exercise contains only two fistfuls of notes

---

EX. 83A

Pat your foot when playing the triplet version on the next page and avoid the mistake of allowing thumb to play louder than the other fingers. If that happens, each thumb note may sound like a downbeat and nobody will know where the time is!

EX. 83B

ETUDE #20

A difficult key like Ab can become an easy key if you conceive your ideas in little fistfuls of notes. Most of the eighth-notes in Etude #20 occur in groups of 4 or 5. Whenever the right hand thumb plays, it's hitting the lowest note of any given "handful" and acts as a kind of navigation beacon.

Upward and Outward

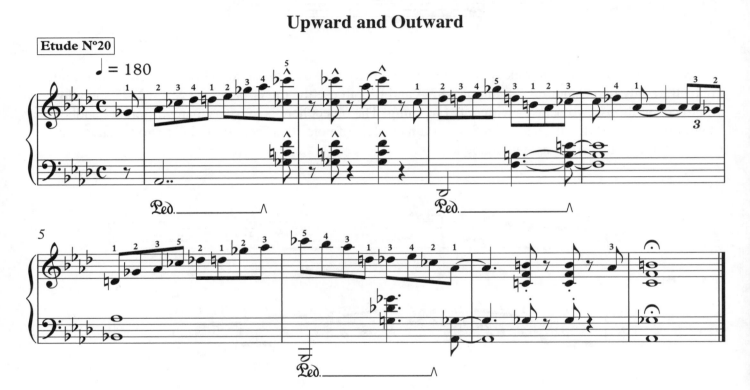

The F# Blues Scale

Ex. 84

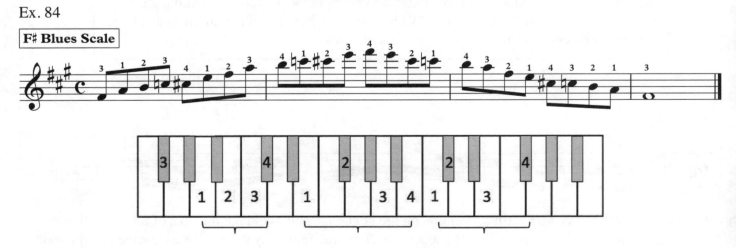

The F# blues scale uses the same simple fingering as Ab: **3 1234 1234 1234**, etc.

Ex. 85 is a blocking exercise. In measures 3 and 4, the thumb always plays the highest note so you have to rotate the hand counterclockwise a bit to tuck the thumb under and allow the other fingers to pass over the top. This exercise is harder to play than the actual scale, which is the point. It's like a baseball player warming up with a weighted bat.

EX. 85

In the triplet version, all the downbeats are either C or F#.

EX. 86A

Ex. 86B has just the downbeats from Ex. 86A, each of which proceeded with its pickup note. No contortions are necessary, just pick up the entire hand and move it to the next pair of notes. If you try for too much legato your hand will get bogged down.

EX. 86B

Ex. 86C allows a one beat resting point between position changes. Use the drop/roll movement in each position to establish a nice, undulating flow.

EX. 86C

Speed Demon #12

Ex. 87A and B below will get you warmed up for Etude #21. Be sure and try adding some left hand chords to add color. Even though this is the F# blues scale, it will also work beautifully with the following chords:

| D major 7th | G major 7th | C major 7th |
| B minor 7th | F# minor | F#7 |

ETUDE #21

The only awkward jump in this etude is where the 4th finger plays two notes in a row at the end of measure two. Always keep mind that odd fingerings are there for the purpose of keeping notes clustered in little handfuls of three or four. Try transposing this piece down a half-step to F minor (four flats.) You'll instantly appreciate how the music that comes naturally to the hand in one key may be almost impossible in another key. *Different geography produces different music.*

The Whale Wins

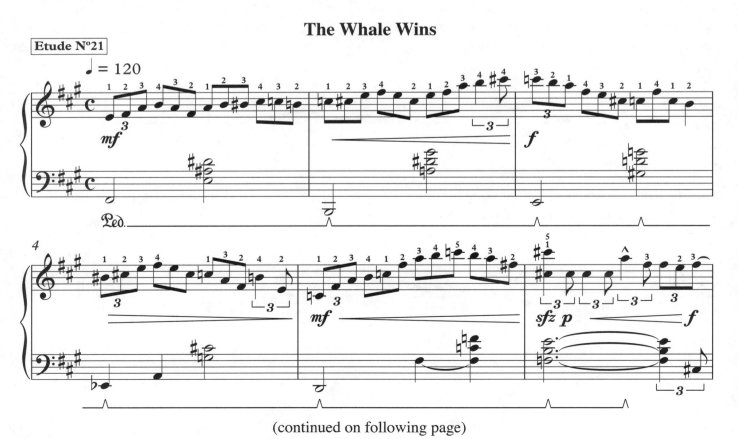

(continued on following page)

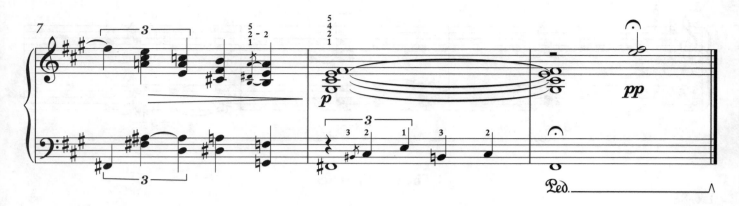

ETUDE #22

Even though Etude #22 uses the F# blues scale, it avoids using any F# chords in the left hand until the final cadence. This is an example of rich, left-hand harmonies coloring a simple right-hand melody.

Perinthia

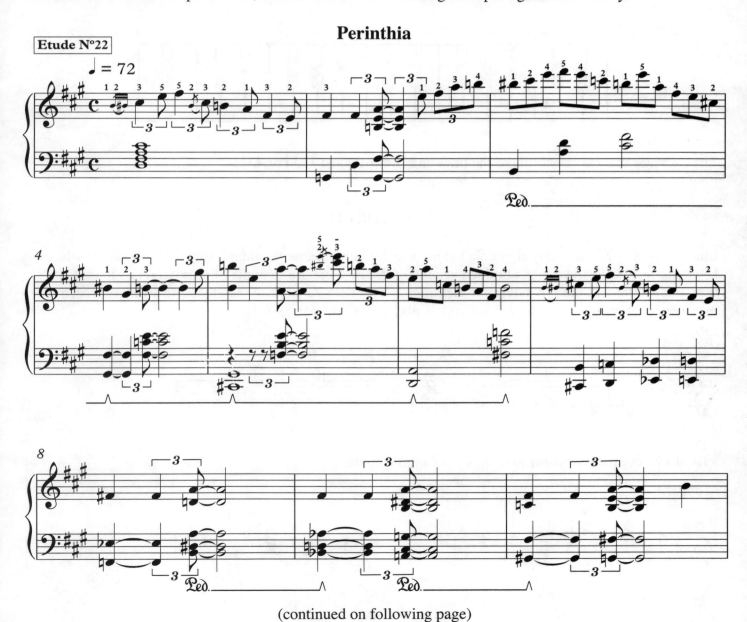

(continued on following page)

The C# Blues Scale

Ex. 88

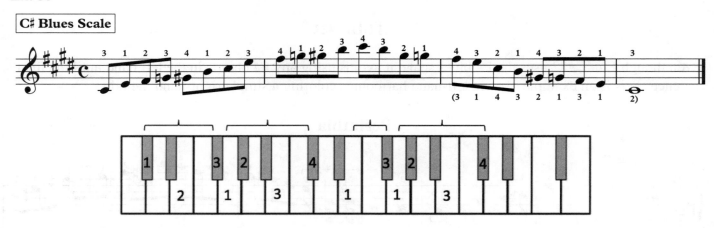

The C# blues scale is easy because the fingering is mostly just **1234** or **4321**.

ETUDE #23

Etudes 23A and 23B are very rhythmic but not too difficult because the thumb stays entirely on the white keys. Etude #23A is the easier, abridged version of #23B. Here are a couple of prep exercises to ease the way. Ex. 89A blocks out the moves for measures 1-2 for both versions of the etude. Be aware that each measure contains one spot where the thumb is playing the highest note.

89B blocks out the moves for measures 3-4 for both etudes.

Promptitude

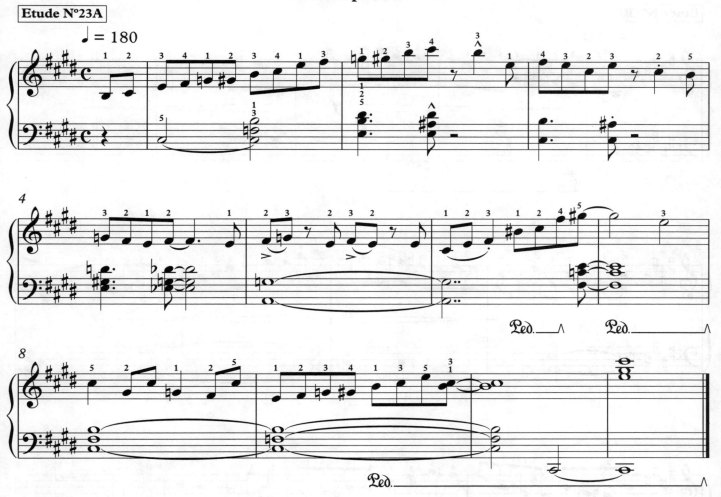

ETUDE #23B

Example 90 blocks out the moves for measures 9 and 10 in Etude 23B.

Promptitude II

Etude Nº23B

110º in the Shade

Chapter 18 - The 12 Blues Scale Fingerings

(Arranged in groups with similar fingerings)

Part V: The Amazing 88 Note Scale

"Just slide your piano bench a foot to the right or left and you can create a whole new emotional vibe."

Wind players can't watch their fingers move. That means that they're free to follow their ears not their eyes. We keyboard players, on the other hand, tend to play only what we can see. This chapter looks at the neglected high and low notes of the piano.

Chapter 19 - The Amazing 88 Note Scale
Colorizing the black and white piano keys

We're taught that there is a twelve-tone scale in western music. This is true only in the sense that there are just twelve basic names for tones, which is reinforced in our hearing by the fact that pitches an octave apart have a similar "quality" or "tone color." But let's ignore the piano for a moment and think of the different timbres produced by a flute or clarinet in their extreme high and low registers. The lowest clarinet notes have a very organic, "woody" sound and the lowest flute notes are mostly air. But as you shift to the highest registers, both instruments "speak" completely differently: the high flute notes sound "silvery" or "brilliant" and high clarinet notes can sound like a pure square wave on an old fashioned synthesizer.

So what is my point?

The point is that since the sound of a wind instrument tends to change character in different registers, there is more of a payoff for a wind player to explore the entire range of that instrument. Another advantage for them is that, unlike pianists, wind players can't even *see* their hands so they do not become visually orient- ed. That means that they're free to follow their ears not their eyes.

We keyboard players, on the other hand, tend to play only what we can see. Unless we're wall-eyed, we can only cast our eyes to the left or right but never both directions simultaneously. This means we dwell in the middle of the keyboard a lot and pray that we never have to hit the highest and lowest keys at the same time! This tunnel vision combined with being armed only twelve names for pitches, can lead to a pianist's view that one octave is pretty much the same and as serviceable as any other. (Notice that I just used the words "see," "vision" and "view.") Our eyes take over from our ears, a kind of deafness to timbres sets in and a lot of beauty gets lost. (The labels we use do affect and limit our view of the world.)

So I'm submitting that the twelve-name system is merely a narrow clerical or bookkeeping convenience that, in a subtle way, can literally narrow a pianist's creative horizons.

Here's an example of what we're talking about. Try playing the "Star Spangled Banner" using only 12 notes as shown in Ex. 91:

EX. 91

Sounds kind of weird, right? A certain lack of completion? You find yourself just craving for that high C to appear and round things out. It turns out then that the sonic message that middle C delivers is NOT the same as the missing C from one octave higher.

Let's look at a more extreme example. Here's some of that famous "shark" music from the movies. Also try playing it down an octave.

Now try raising it up several octaves:

Whoaa…the "same" notes carry a completely different message. Sounds more like a little, pink, bathtub shark rather than a leviathan from the deep! This is the concept that pianists need to absorb: the piano actually contains a giant 88 note scale, not just a single, 12 note scale that is cloned out seven times across the keys.

To illustrate that point, example 93 below runs a single three-note idea up and down the keyboard. Some players might feel like it's "cheating" when you merely transpose an idea through different octaves, but the joke is on them: it's actually a bit difficult for the ear to tell that they ARE the "same" notes. In this case, the ear wins: they, in fact, are not the same: they only share the same letter names.

Example 94 below uses some of the highest range of the piano to convey…what? Perhaps heat waves shimmering in the desert or maybe an ocean fog rolling in? This mood could have only been conceived in the upper register and if you transpose it down an octave or two it becomes a different piece. Neglecting this high range sends away a whole galaxy of emotions that can't be articulated through the middle or low ranges of the piano. Use the sustain-pedal freely—the idea is to produce a kind of sonic haze.

EX. 94

In example 95, we leave the high register and head down into the basement to explore the deep, rich, oily, teakwood sounds of the blues. Whereas Ex. 94 above was all higher than middle C, Ex. 95 is mostly lower. You can create an entirely different emotional vibe by simply sliding your piano bench about twelve inches to the left!

EX. 95

(continued on following page)

Example 95B dramatically blends both the high and low registers.

(continued on following page)

Hold on to that idea of the 88 Note Scale because we'll be using of that concept in the rest of this book. Just think of it as a way to colorize your ideas, just as the movie studios colorize vintage black and white movies.

Break the Mold
You should take every etude and little exercise in this book and transpose it either up or down an octave to the next adjacent register. The results can be comical but can also accidentally lead you to totally new sound palettes.

Part VI: The Coltrane Pentatonic Scale

This section will introduce a variation of the major pentatonic scale that contains the important interval of a tritone.

Chapter 20 - The Coltrane Pentatonic Scale

Introducing the "Coltrane" Scale

In the next couple of chapters we'll look at two very cool "altered" scales, each being a slight alteration of the major pentatonic scale. What makes these two scales similar (and awesome too) is that each contains the interval of a *tritone*, which is a distance of three whole steps (going either up or down the keyboard.) An example of the tritone interval would be the notes E to Bb or Bb to F flat as shown in Ex. 96 (that strange F flat will be explained in Ex. 97.)

Ex. 96

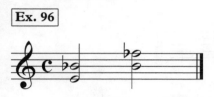

The interval of a tritone happens to be the heart and soul of the dominant 7th chord. That means that any scale that has a tritone lurking somewhere in it will work beautifully over a dominant 7th chord.

The reason for this is that the identity and basic character of any chord is determined by what the 3rd and 7th scale degrees are. They are called the *modal tones*. If they happen to be a tritone apart, then that chord will be a dominant seventh. If you take the tritones from Ex. 96 and put them in that context (as in in Ex. 97 below) you will get two different dominant 7th chords:

Ex. 97

(The reason the note E is replaced with an F flat in Ex. 97 is just for clerical reasons. It allows the Gb7 chord to remain spelled as a stack of thirds. We tend to read chord shapes, not individual notes within the shapes.)

This tritone interval is a very "active" interval and just cries out for resolution. That's just a way of saying that it has a strong pulling force and creates a rich, opulent character in a scale or chord. The shocking fact is that the major and minor pentatonics we've already looked at contain no tritones- they were all derived from a stack of perfect fourths. That makes them very passive sounding if you don't some add rich, bluesy harmonies with the left hand. The effect of including a tritone in a scale will become immediately apparent below as we examine the "Coltrane" pentatonic scale.

> ### The "Coltrane" Major Pentatonic Scale (aka the 1, 2, 3, 5, b7 scale)
> The first of our two altered pentatonic scales is one used by many jazz players, including John Coltrane, Wes Montgomery and McCoy Tyner. It is simply a major pentatonic scale with the last note raised up a half-step to become the lowered 7th instead of the 6th.

Major pentatonic   "Coltrane" pentatonic

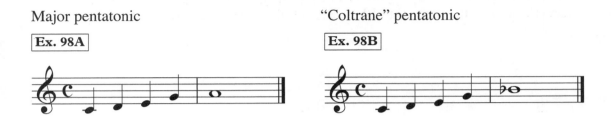

An amazing fact about this scale is that it is just a simple rearrangement of the five notes found in a dominant 9th chord.

If you look the basic model of a C ninth chord in Ex. 99, the stack of thirds you see there gives little indication of the cool scale that resides in it. Just lower the top note D down an octave and what you get is a tightly bunched stack of notes…fairly useless until you unfold it as a scale. Your playing will practically shout out "ninth chord" whenever you use it!

Another cool aspect of the "Coltrane" pentatonic is that if you attempt to arrange it into a stack of perfect fourths (as you can do with the major pentatonic scale), you'll find that most of the fourths have disappeared but you end up with richer, bluesy chord.

In Ex. 100 measures 1-3 show the sound of a regular C major pentatonic scale arranged into a stack of fourths. Measures 3-6 show the Coltrane pentatonic arranged the same way. When the note "A" in the first measure is changed to Bb in measure four, *presto*, the sound has instantly become a warm, dominant 9th chord. Use lots of sustain pedal to bring this effect out.

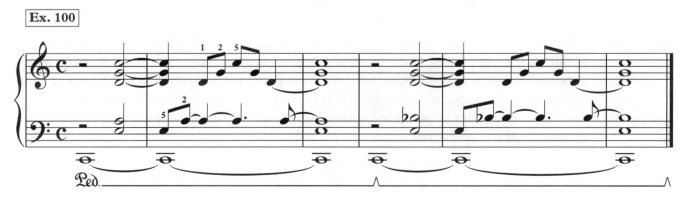

Chapter 21 - The C, F, G, Bb and D Coltrane Scales

Coltrane Pentatonic Scale in C

We'll start with the four scales C, F, G and D because they have nearly identical fingerings. Learn these and you will then be prepared to try them out in Etudes 25 and 26 which follow.

Ex. 101 - C Major (b7)

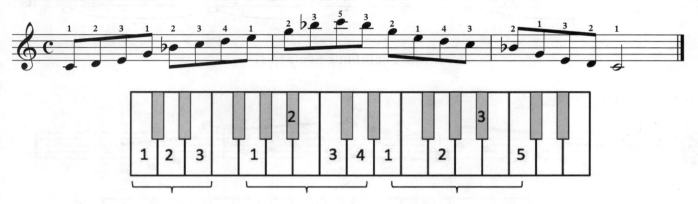

Extended Exercise in C

Coltrane Pentatonic Scale in F

Ex. 103 - F Major (b7)

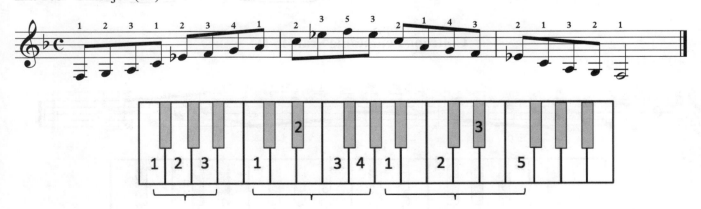

108

Extended Exercise in F

Ex. 104

Coltrane Pentatonic Scale in G

Ex. 105 - G Major (b7)

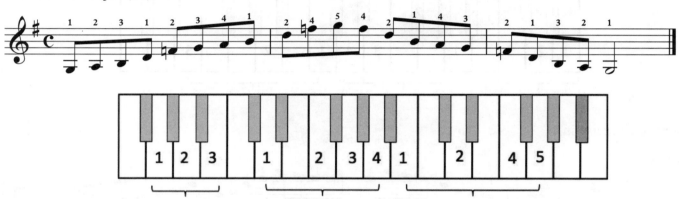

Extended Exercise in G

Ex. 106

Coltrane Pentatonic Scale in D

Ex. 107 - D Major (b7)

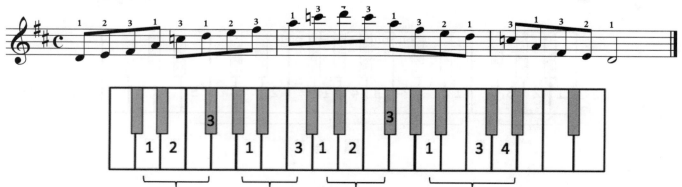

Extended Exercise in D

Ex. 108

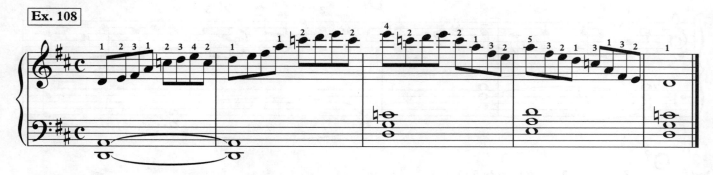

ETUDE #25

Etude #25 uses the C, D and G Coltrane scales. It is based on the harmonies of Duke Ellington's "Take The A Train.".It is followed by three prep exercises. Pardon my ending chord.

Take A Train

Etude Nº 25

(continued on next page)

Prep Exercises for Etude #25

Ex. 109 blocks out measures 5 and 6.

Ex. 110 blocks out measures 11 and 12.

Ex. 111 blocks out measures 13 and 14.

ETUDE #26

Etude #26 uses the Coltrane scale based on F and Bb. If you have difficulties with the rhythm in the first two measures, Ex. 112 at the bottom of this Etude will help smooth things out for you.

1958

Prep Exercise for Etude #26

112

Coltrane Pentatonic Scale in Bb

Ex. 113 – Bb Major (b7)

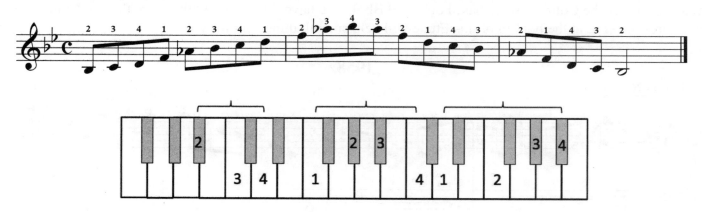

If the Bb scale feels a bit awkward because it starts with the 2nd finger, just ignore the first three notes and practice beginning with the thumb on F as shown in Ex. 114. When you're ready, go back to Ex. 113 and add the missing three notes from the beginning.

Ex. 114

Extended Exercise in Bb

EX. 115

ETUDE #27

This Etude #27 uses the Bb, C and F Coltrane scales. It is followed by a prep exercise that addresses measures 1 and 2.

Take Another Train

Prep Exercise for Etude #27

Ex. 116 blocks out the first two measures. Be aware that, in the measure #1 below, the thumb plays a higher note than the 3rd finger does.

Chapter 22 - The A and E Coltrane Scales

We'll now add the A and E scales to our repertory which will prepare the hand for Etude 28.

Coltrane Scale in A

Ex. 117 – A Major

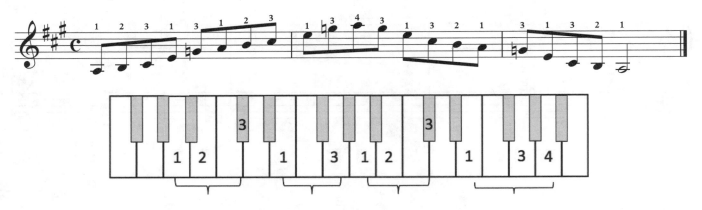

Extended Exercise in A

Ex. 118

Coltrane Scale in E

Ex. 119 – E Major

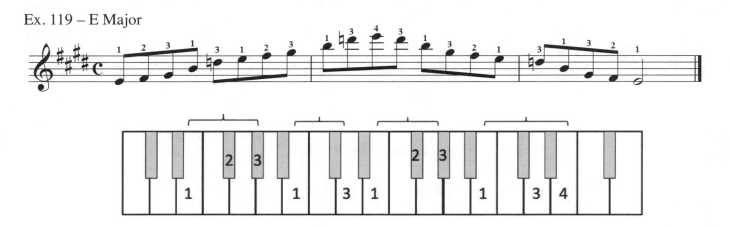

Extended Exercise in E

ETUDE #28

Etude 28 introduces the Coltrane scales in A and E and also reviews the G, C and F scales. The letters beneath the bass clef indicate which scale is being quoted.

Alicia's Star

(continued on following page)

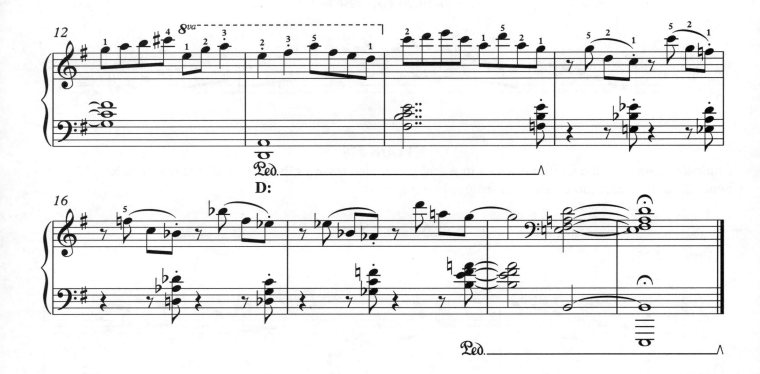

Chapter 23 - The Eb and Ab Coltrane Scales

Ex. 121 – Eb Major

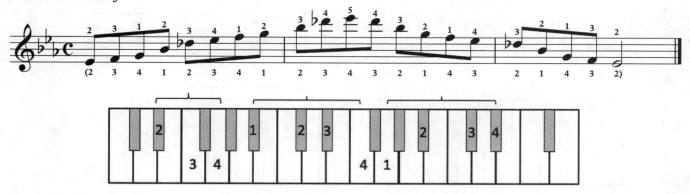

Extended Exercise in Eb

Ex. 122A

Example 122A above requires the thumb to be way in over the black keys. 122B and C choreograph out the weird hand positions that the scale generates.

In example 122B, your fingers should be almost touching the backboard!

Ex. 122B

Ex. 122C adds an upper harmony note to the ones you practiced in Ex. 122B.

Ex. 122C

Coltrane Scale in Ab

Ex. 123 – Ab Major

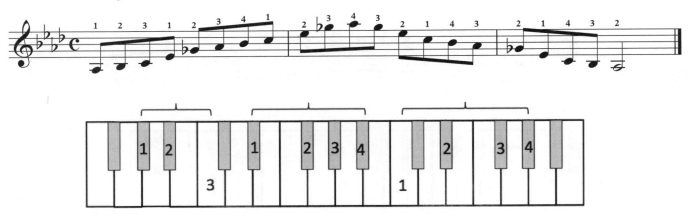

Extended Exercise in Ab

Ex. 124A

Exercise 124A above requires the thumb to be way in over the black keys. 124B and C help choreograph out the awkward hand positions that the Ab scale generates.

Ex. 124B

Ex. 124C

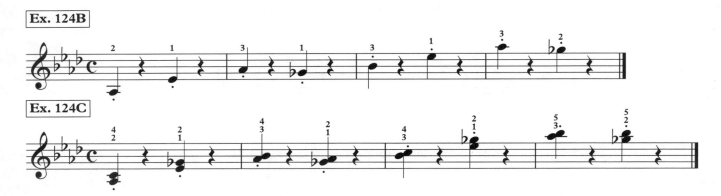

ETUDE #29

Etude 29 (on the following page) uses the Eb and Ab Coltrane pentatonic scales and also reviews the Bb scale too.

Thad and Mel

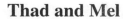

Etude N° 29

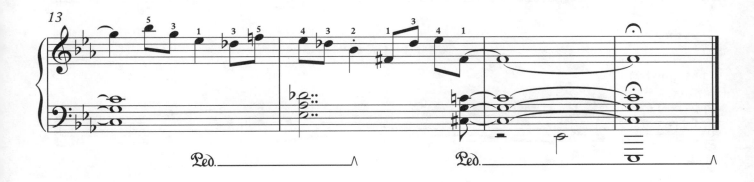

Chapter 24 - Review of the Coltrane Scale Fingerings

(Arranged in groups with similar fingerings)

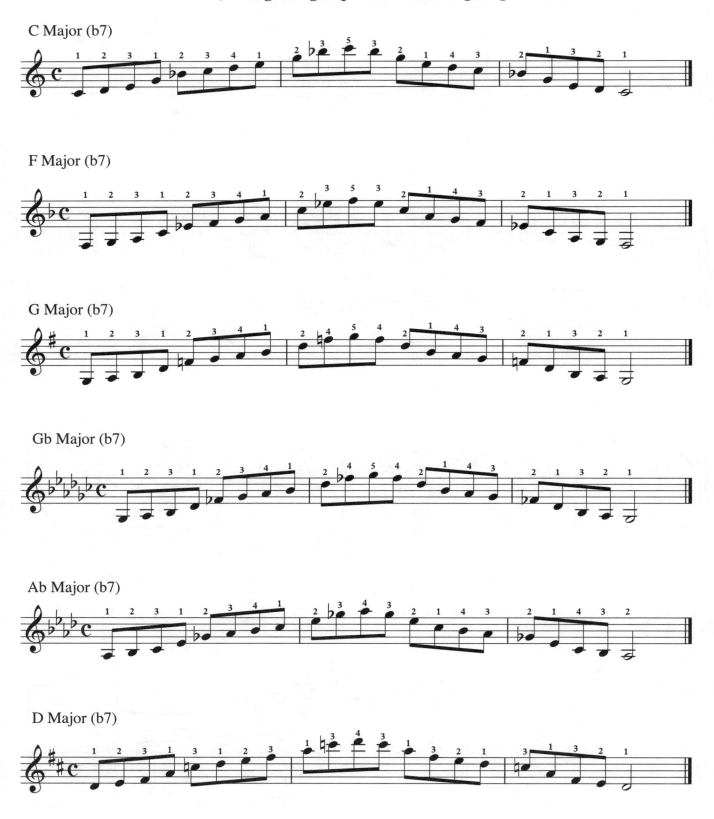

A Major (b7)

E Major (b7)

Eb Major (b7)

Db Major (b7)

Bb Major (b7)

B Major (b7)

Part VII:
The Amazing Flatted-6th Pentatonic Scale

This is the first and only scale in this book that contains the interval of a minor 2nd. It's impossible to create a real dissonance without either that interval or its inversion, the major 7th.

Chapter 25 - The Major Flatted-6th Pentatonic Scale

Intro to the Amazing 1, 2, 3, 5, b6 Major Scale

This is the second of the two altered pentatonic scales mentioned earlier in this book and the final scale we'll look at before moving on to how to be creative with all these materials.

I don't have an official name for the new scale here other than the flat 6th or Major b6 pentatonic scale. It's similar to the Coltrane pentatonic except that the sixth degree is lowered a half step instead of being raised. Here is an example built on C:

The hidden dynamite in this scale is that it introduces a half-step interval into the pentatonic family. That would be the G to Ab in the example above.

So, what's the big deal about a half step?

To the modern ear, it's virtually impossible to perceive a single chord or interval as being "dissonant" unless it contains a half-step or one of its inversions. Here's that G to Ab half-step followed by two inversions. The sound may give you a toothache but I'm pretty sure that it's impossible to construct a dissonance without them!

There is another even greater gem hidden in the flat 6th scale: it contains the interval of a tritone, just as the Coltrane, flatted 7th pentatonic did.

Ex. 127A shows our new tritone interval (D-Ab) found in the C version of the flat 6th scale. Ex. 127B then shows the three, basic, everyday chords (Bb7, F minor 6th and E7) that contain that particular tritone.

So, Is This Thing Really a "C" Scale, or What...?

An excellent question.

You may have noticed that, even though Ex. 127 was advertised as a type of C *scale*, that no mention was made of any C *chords*. Oops! So before you take it at face value that it is merely a C scale with an Ab perched on top, let's perform a litmus test: let's try to rearrange the notes to form a stack of perfect fourths as we did in the C major pentatonic scale.

Ex. 128A is the fourth-stack we pulled out of the C Major pentatonic scale mentioned earlier in the book. Then example 128B shows our new C flat 6th scale, rearranged into the same kind of stack. *Voila!* The simple act of lowering of the A to become an Ab (or G#) creates an entirely new chord!

C major pentatonic   C-flatted 6th pentatonic

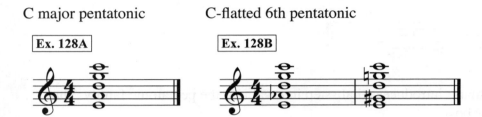

As you can see, the C major, flatted 6th fourth-stack plainly reveals itself to be an E7 (#9th) chord! This scale perfectly expresses so many chords that are not "C" (such as E7, Bb7, F minor or A minor) that calling it a "C" scale is merely a name of convenience.

This is a very rich sound to explore and Example 129 gives you an isolated example. It begins with the C major pentatonic as a scale and then is rearranged into a fourth stack for comparison. Then it demonstrates how the C major, flat 6th scale can be used over an E7 chord too, which resolves nicely to the key of A minor at the end. We'll also use this scale against other chords here shortly.

The brilliant thing about the presence of both the tritone and the half-step interval is that we now have our first scale that contains a full complement of notes that can create full, modern sounding chords, all filled out with a 3rd, 7th and some color tones left over.

Here are some chords constructed from just the five notes in the C-flatted 6th scale. In some cases (such as Bb13) the bass note isn't actually in the scale. Again, the point here is that the powerful interval of a tritone found in our "C" scale expresses so many things not "C."

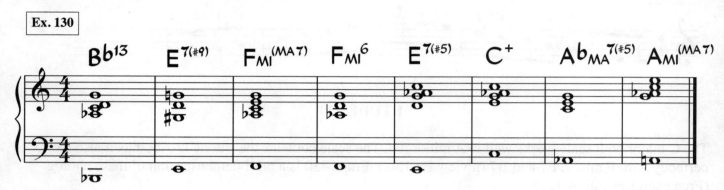

We'll have fun with these and many other rich sounding chords in chapter 16 as we try them out with all of the twelve flatted 6th scales.

Chapter 26 - Meet the Major Flatted-6th Scales

The C, F, D and G Major b6th Scales

The major scale with a flatted 6th that is built on C is easy to learn because it uses the same fingering as the plain C major pentatonic.

C major b6

ETUDE #30

The C major b6th scale works well in A minor too. The scale contains the tritone D-Ab, thus it also works perfectly with F minor, E7 and B7 (review Ex.130.) Etude #30 is a brief demonstration of these chords. (Prep exercises follow.)

Now and Then

(continued on following page)

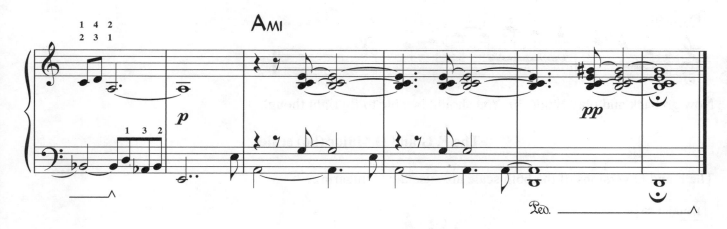

Prep Exercises for Etude #30

In staying consistent with our concept of thinking "away to," Ex. 131A and B will bypass the first three measures of Etude 30 and begin with the second hand-position of the C major b6th scale from measure four. The half-notes are the downbeats and the stem-down quarter-notes are just to be tapped lightly. Don't use any thumb-under moves here…just hop the entire arm over for the final two notes.

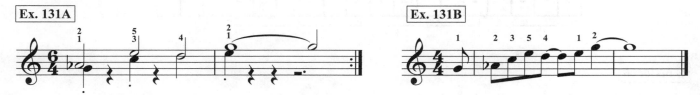

In Ex. 132 we tunnel backwards to measure three of the etude connect it to measure four. Don't think about measure three too hard as you play it—be thinking only of measure four that follows.

Ex. 133 is from measure five. It's a bit tricky because it involves three hand positions in just six beats. Notice also that the thumb switches from playing the lowest note to become the highest in the first measure…ouch!

Ex. 133B

Now go back and play Etude 30. You should be able to fly right though it.

The F, G and D Major (b6) scales

The F and G versions of the b6th scale also use the C fingering.

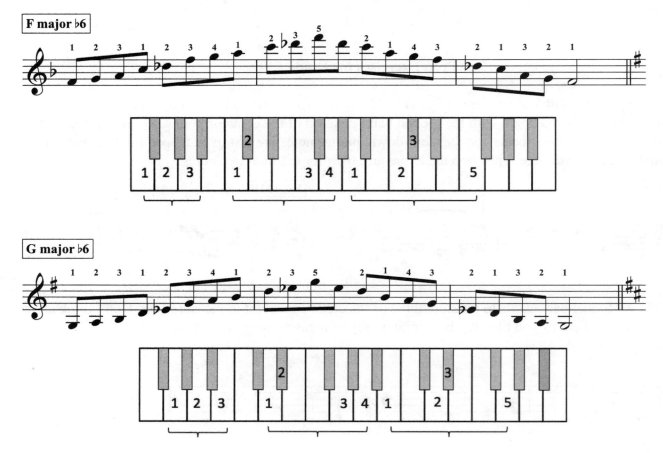

F major ♭6

G major ♭6

The geography of the D scale is a bit trickier because the presence of two black keys throws the hand off a bit. This requires that we use four hand positions instead of three.

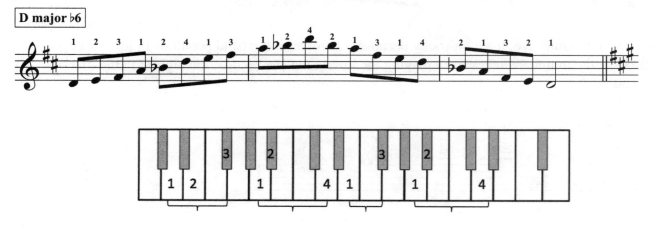

D major ♭6

ETUDE #31

Etude #31 will use all four of the flat 6th scales that have been discussed so far—G, D, C and F. They will appear in that exact order and will be colored by chords that have different roots than the actual scale used.

The flat 6th scale is like a chameleon blending into a landscape. It takes on the coloration of so many rich chords that, for now, we will deal only with the specific ones found in Etude 31.

In Ex. 134 we see how the G Major (b6) scale fits in with both an E minor and a C minor chord. If you sense a certain moodiness or sultriness in the sound, it's because the raised 7th (as opposed to the lowered or dominant 7th) keeps cropping up. Minor chords with the raised 7th are used to great effect in classic *noir* movies and also in James Bond films too. The example below uses the chords from the first two measures of Etude 31.

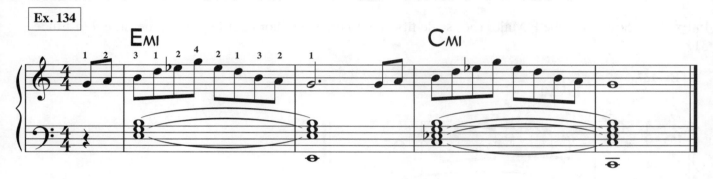

Ex. 135 shows how the D Major (b6) scale fits in with both a G minor and a Bb augmented chord. If your chord symbol knowledge is rusty, just remember that "augment" means making something larger. In music that means making a chord a bit wider by raising the 5th a half-step. In a Bb chord that means you raise the F up to an F#.

Both chords shown below continue the moodiness…in the G minor that's caused by the raised 7th (F#) and in the Bb chord it's the F# again (that's the augmented note mentioned above.) These chords are found in measures 3 and 4 of Etude 31.

Ex. 136 shows how the C Major (b6) scale fits in with an A minor, F minor and an E7(#5) chord. These chords are found in measures 6-8 of Etude 31.

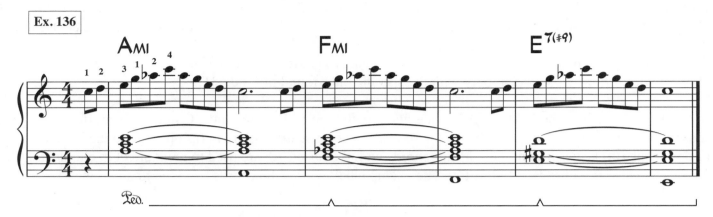

In Ex. 137 shows how the F Major (b6) scale fits in with the Bb minor chord found in measure 9 of Etude 31.

How to Spot a Flat 6th Pentatonic Scale

Sometimes I'll casually glance at Etudes 31 or 32 and go, "Uhm, er, what flat 6th scale is this that I'm looking at right now?" That's understandable because in a long string of notes you can become confused from seeing so many tones common to other scales.

*The answer is: **Look for a half-step interval. It always defines the 5th and flatted 6th of a given scale.** Remember, none of the four pentatonic scales in this book contains a half-step except for this flat-6th scale.*

ETUDE #31

Etude 31 (on the following page) has a walking tempo, swing feel. Observe the pedal marks carefully because they're there to generate gentle washes of sound. Learn the left hand with the pedal first to get a balanced sound and then add the right hand later. The G, D, C and F flat 6th scales appear in that order. Can you identify them?

The Poet

Etude Nº31

Chapter 27 - The A, Bb, B and F# Major Flatted-6th Scales

Etude #32 will incorporate four new major (b6) scales into the mix. Before we get to that etude, here's a rundown of the four new scales. They involve a variety of fingerings, which, if you practice them well, should put you at ease with a whole new world of tactile patterns that you may have previously found intimidating. That is, of course, the ultimate purpose of this book.

A Major (b6)

The A major (b6) scale uses the same fingering as D.

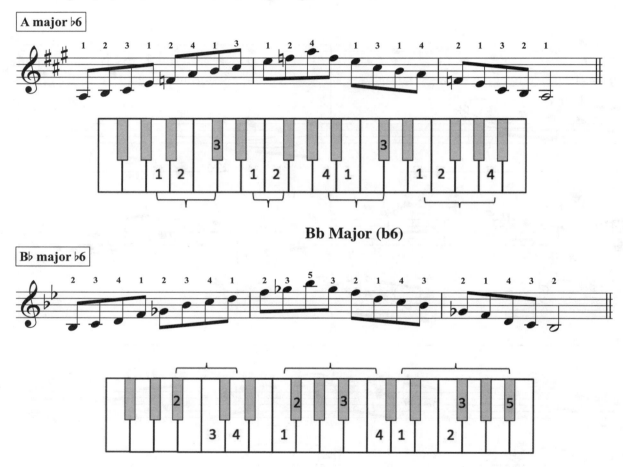

Bb Major (b6)

As you may notice, the most difficult part of the Bb scale is the first few notes. In Ex. 138 we'll just ignore them for a moment and start by practicing on the second hand position first.

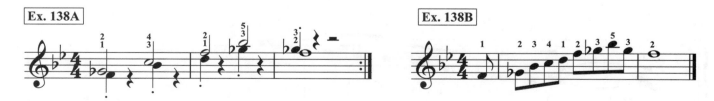

Now we'll go back and start at the beginning of the scale and attack that first hand position. Example 139 on the following page starts out with only the downbeats. It always amazes me how piano playing is often more about just throwing the hand around the keyboard rather than using the fingers.

Ex. 139

Example 140 blocks out the descending hand positions found in the lowest octave of the scale. Be aware that the thumb is playing the highest note at the beginning of the fourth measure. If your hand feels stiff in this exercise, you need to keep practicing it until you feel no resistance. Thinking "away to" and anticipating how your hand has to move to accommodate the next position is more mental than physical. A millisecond's hesitation in "letting go" when you want to move on can create the illusion that you have slow fingers.

Ex. 140

Here's a final run through of the scale:

B Major (b6)

The B scale offers two basic fingering choices. The fingering just above the notes makes the first measure fairly easy but the rest becomes a bit awkward. The alternate fingering does the reverse—measure one becomes a challenge but there's smooth sailing after that in the last two measures.

B major ♭6

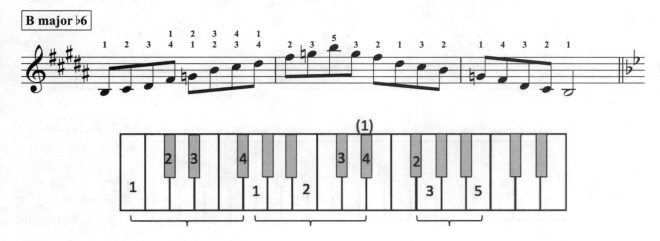

134

As usual, we'll begin practicing the second hand position first. Ex. 141 begins with the thumb plays the highest note G.

Ex. 141

Now we'll go back and start at the beginning of the scale with the first hand position.

Ex. 142

Example 143 blocks out the hand positions for the descending portion of the B scale.

Ex. 143

Here's a final runthrough.

Gb Major (b6)

Examples 144 through 154 will use the keys of "Gb" and "F#" interchangeably. This will avoid having to use lots of double flats and sharps.

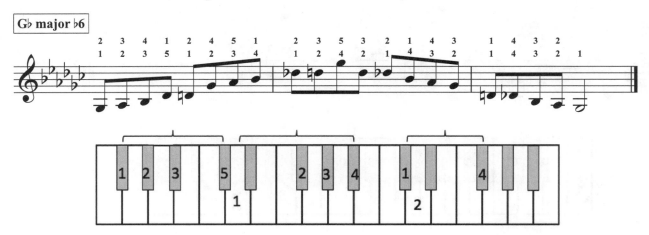

Ex. 144 blocks out the second hand position of the F# (b6) scale. Note that the first note is D played by the thumb *above* the C#.

Ex. 144

In Ex. 145 keep the thumb in over the two notes it has to play.

Ex. 145

Ex. 146 requires only two hand positions.

Ex. 146

Now we'll go back and start at the beginning of the F# b6th scale. The half-notes here are the downbeats of the F# scale. If you keep the hand way in over the black keys, this will prepare you to fly through Ex. 148.

Ex. 147

Ex. 148

In Ex. 148 above, the thumb got to play lots of downbeats. It does that very well because it's naturally clumsy. The triplet pattern in Ex. 149 on the following page lets other fingers play the downbeats and forces that aggressive thumb to back off and play with a lighter touch.

Ex. 149

Example 150 blocks out the hand positions for descending portion of the F# scale. All the half-notes (and the thumb too) occur on the downbeats so this should be fairly easy to play.

Ex. 150

In Ex. 151 the recurring fingering pattern **4321 4321** makes traveling downward pretty easy.

Ex. 151

The triplets in Ex. 152 can fool the eye (and the hand) into forgetting that all these notes are just three simple finger groups: 12421 4321 4321. Keep the thumb way in—that will give it the stability and control to avoid it playing too loudly. If necessary, go back and review Ex. 150.

Ex. 152

Ex. 153 outlines the downbeats for the entire two-octave F# (b6) scale. How fast can you play this? The thumb plays 8 out the 11 notes here so keep your elbow loose and let it guide your thumb in and out of the keys.

Ex. 153

In our final run through below, notice that every time the left hand plays a chord that the right hand thumb is playing too.

ETUDE #32

Etude #32 will now make use of the four, flatted 6th scales that we've just studied: A, Bb, B and F# (or Gb). They will appear in that exact order and will be colored by chords that have different roots than the actual scale used. Ex. 155-60 shows how.

1) Ex. 155 shows how the first four measures of Etude 32 use the **A Major (b6)** scale over a D minor chord. This shows how you *don't* let a chord name totally dictate what notes you are playing (this also occurs in measures 13 through 16).

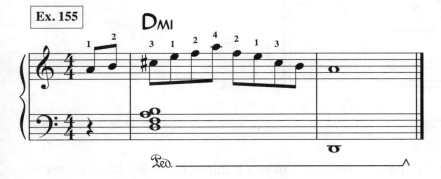

2) Ex. 156 shows how measures 5-7 of Etude 32 make use of the **G Major (b6)** scale over a C minor chord. Then in measure 19 it used over a B augmented 7th chord. What unites them is the tritone interval of Eb to A found in both chords.

3) Ex. 157 shows how measure 8 of Etude 32 uses the Bb Major (b6) scale over a D7 chord and then how the final three measures then use it over an Eb minor 6th chord. What unites them is the tritone C to Gb. It is the essential color tones of both chords.

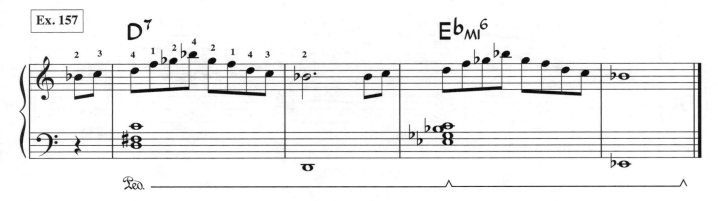

4) Ex. 158 shows how measures 11-12 use F Major (b6) scale over an A+7 chord. What unites them is that *every tone* in this F scale (except for C) is an essential color tone of an A+7.

5) Ex. 159 shows how measures 20-21 use the B Major (b6) scale over a E minor #7 chord. What unites them is that *every tone* in this B scale (except for C#) is an essential color tone of an E minor #7.

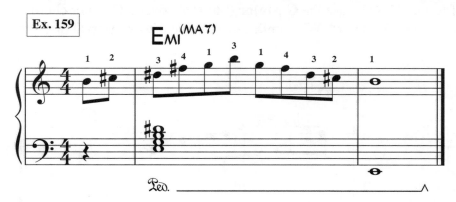

6) Ex. 160 on the following page shows how measures 24-26 use F# Major (b6) scale over a B minor #7 chord. What unites them is that *every tone* in this F# scale (except for A#) is an essential color tone of a B minor #7.

Ex. 160

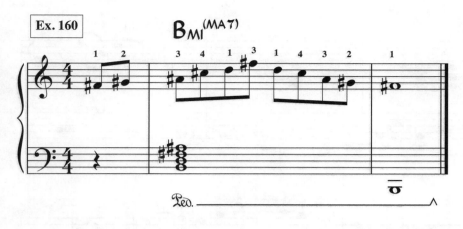

ETUDE #32

Question: A quick look at Etude 32 reveals a half-step in measure 3, a different one leading into measure 5 and yet another one in measure 8. Can you ID what three scales they are from?

This etude moves quite freely around the keyboard. Six out of every ten notes here are played by the thumb and index fingers, usually in combination, so, for gosh sake, keep the that thumb in over the knuckle.

The East Village

Chapter 28 - Review of the Major Flat-6th Scale Fingerings
(Arranged in groups with similar fingerings)

142

Part VIII: Creativity

"This chapter isn't about more scales; it's all about chord shapes. The more shapes you have, the more freedom there is."

Chapter 29 - Creativity

THREE NOTE CHORD SHAPES

> *This chapter isn't about more scales; it's all about shapes.*
> *The more shapes you have, the more freedom there is.*
>
> Imagine an instrument with only five notes. You couldn't really make much music by running scale passages up and down those notes because there just aren't enough of them. It suddenly becomes all about the contours and rhythms you create from the chord shapes that the hand has learned.

So now that you know something about the anatomies of four pentatonic scales and the blues scale, we need to find some ways to make music with them. You may have already discovered that running up and down all 60 scales is interesting for a while but then things start getting old pretty fast. Scales are of very limited use, at least until the chance encounter where some musical phrase requires the same notes with identical fingerings. In other words, you need to break away from the scales before you end up just quoting them verbatim because that's all that the hand knows. In classical music the composer "thinks up" music and that process dictates whether or not scales are quoted. But when improvising your own music, the hand tends to dictate as much as the head does.

So, how do we begin? Good question—glad you asked.

We begin by severely limiting ourselves.

We've started with the pentatonic scale, which already excludes seven notes out of the twelve available to us and now we'll exclude even two more. This will reduce our inventory to just three notes. Then there's little else to do but work in some rhythms to bring what's left to life. The best way to start is with a fourth stack and it's two inversions. This chord is the basic triad that "speaks" the pentatonic language in the same manner that major or minor triads made up of thirds "speak" the traditional European major/minor system.

ROOT POSITION FOURTH STACKS

A basic fact of life about the major and minor pentatonic scales emerges when you see that they can be laid out in a stack of perfect fourths. As a reminder, we'll start by taking the all-black, Gb major scale and arranging it into fourths by starting on Bb. Keep in mind that this is the Eb minor pentatonic scale too.

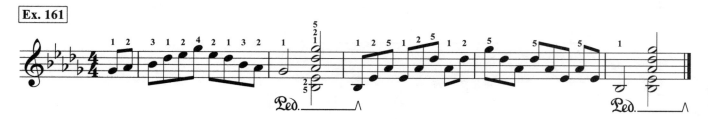

Ex. 161

Ex. 162A has just the downbeats from measures 3 to 5 of example 161 above. It's amazing that just getting your hand over that darned repeated Ab is the secret to playing these stacks of fourths…six out nine notes are the same Ab!

Ex. 162A

Now we block out the positions for all of the notes in measures 3 to 5 of Ex. 161. Lean the weight of the hand toward the half-note and away from whichever side the quarter note is on.

Ex. 162B

Now go back and play through Ex. 161 until you're comfortable with running up and down those fourth-stacks. If the hand isn't relaxed on the black keys, it will just stiffen up when you move on to two full octaves in Ex. 163 A and B.

Ex. 163A blocks out two full octaves of the fourth stacks contained in the G scale.

Ex. 163A

Ex. 163B is merely a single-note version of the chords you just practiced above. It may look a bit confusing and even intimidating but that's the cool part. If you glance at it with no reference to the simple fingerings attached, it almost looks like a random sequence of black keys. People will think you're much smarter than you actually are…ha! Actually, it's the left hand chords that are random…almost all chords seem to work with a pentatonic scale.

Ex. 163B

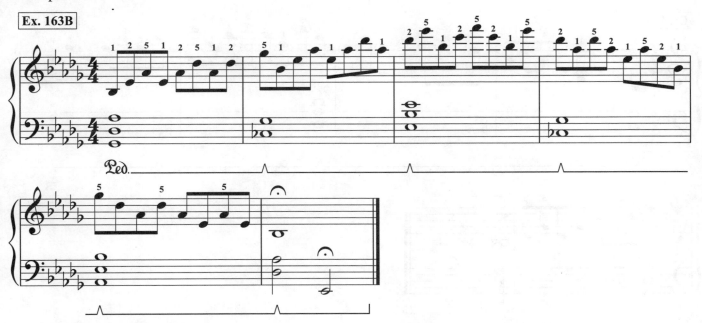

Now, for variety, take everything you just did on the black keys in Ex. 161-163 and move it all down a half-step to the F major/ D minor pentatonic scale. This will create and all-white fourth stack built up from A.

Ex. 164

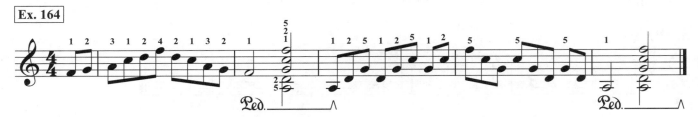

Here are just the downbeats from measures 3-5 in Ex. 164. Six out of the nine notes are G!

Ex. 165A

Ex. 165B blocks out the positions for all of the fourth stacks in example 164. Lean the weight of the hand toward the half-note and away from whichever side the quarter note is on.

Ex. 165B

Ex. 166A blocks out two full octaves of the fourth stacks contained in the F major pentatonic scale. It's all white keys…so play with your eyes closed!

Ex. 166A

Here is a single-note version of the chords you just practiced above.

Ex. 166B

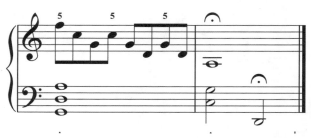

TRANSPOSING CHALLENGE

Now go back and transpose exercises 164-66 up one step to become the G major/E minor pentatonic. It's all white keys again so you may have to practice with eyes closed to avoid getting lost! Just keep in mind all the great players who didn't have the benefit of any eyesight at all: Art Tatum, Ray Charles, George Shearing, Stevie Wonder and Lennie Tristano.

INVERTING THE FOURTH STACK

Ok, enough with the root position fourth-stacks. We'll now arbitrarily select the "G" stack and invert it and see what intriguing chords might emerge. These shapes will be also used to create the single-note lines we'll be using.

Ex. 167A

The chords above are built from the thumb up, so Ex. 167B works on just the lowest two notes of each shape first.

Ex. 167B

Ex. 167C works the weaker 4th and 5th fingers on the upper two notes.

Ex. 167C

Now return to Ex. 167A and see if it feels more secure.

Ex. 168 breaks down the chords from Ex. 167A into single notes to complete the process.

Ex. 168

What's in a Name?

We won't name the fourth stack inversions we've just discussed just yet because they are literally everything! Even at a glance, Ex. 169 shows that the C-F-G stack can be a chameleon. It simultaneously spells out 2/3 of a C chord, an F chord and a G7. …it also resembles C minor and F minor too!

To add to the confusion, the notes C, F and G contained in our "G" fourth-stack are also three of the five notes found in the C, D and G minor pentatonic scales. In addition, they also make up three out of the five notes in the F, Bb and Eb *major* pentatonics.

Wait, there's more. The first and second inversions of our G fourth stack are also the heart of the Ab Major 7th and a Db Major 7th chords (Ex. 170 below). In addition, they outline an A minor 7th and D minor 7th too! To my ears, the sudden shifts of color in Ex. 170 almost suggest a lyric song.

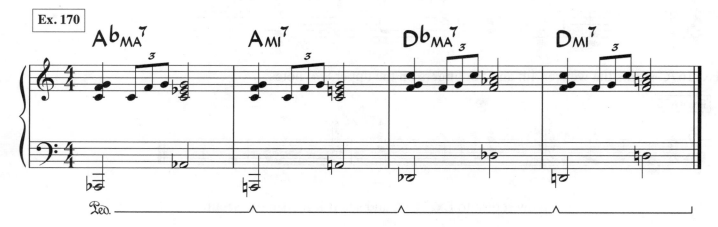

Okay, so this chapter has examined the fingerings and a few of the harmonic possibilities of a simple stack of fourths built on G. In Chapter 30 we'll move on to the rhythmic aspect, which is what makes jazz unique.

Chapter 30 - Eighty Eight Drums

Adding Rhythms

> *Too many jazz players just search for "interesting" notes, which is a very European concept. Another approach is to assume that the notes you play will have limited melodic or harmonic value, but will instead act as vehicles to express rhythms. Each piano key will become a little tuned drum.*

Much of the music below, from Example 172 all the way through Etude 33, may seem repetitious and a bit limited, but the lesson here is how to choose a small number of notes and then "work" them rhythmically to develop ideas. *These notes have little melodic value but are vehicles to express rhythms. Each piano key is a little tuned drum.*

Now that we've seen how just a few notes can imply many different chords let's look at how interesting and coherent rhythms can also color the notes. Examples 172-176 will walk you through a series of four rhythmic variations while just using the notes **C-F-G**. Each exercise features one basic jazz rhythm with some harmonies thrown in to brighten things a bit.

If you learn these well, you should hear them running through your head while trying to go to sleep (hopefully in a good way!)

Let's start with the basic, jazz cymbal beat which is a quarter-note followed by two eighth-notes:

Ex. 171A

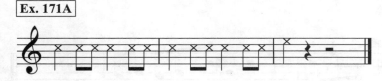

Just to be contrary, let's also reverse that rhythm…

Ex. 171B

and then use that reversed rhythm as in Ex. 172:

Ex. 172

150

Here's a slight variation of the rhythm we used in Ex.172:

If you can sing the rhythm above comfortably plus keep your thumb under control too, then Ex. 174 should flow easily. Try transposing the right hand of Ex. 174 up a half-step (it's all black keys.) If you mentally erase the four flats in the key signature and replace it with three sharps, you can easily play both hands. I used some colorful harmonies to relieve some of the bleakness of all these penatonic scales. This example uses the same notes as Ex. 172.

In Ex. 175, three note groups create some nice cross-rhythms. Rhythms used in this manner create what is known as an *agogic* accent. That means a melodic accent. In other words, there's nothing here except a boring stream of 1/8th notes, but the melodic contours themselves create little accents. Again, we're reusing the same notes from Ex. 172-174. Kind of hard to tell, right?

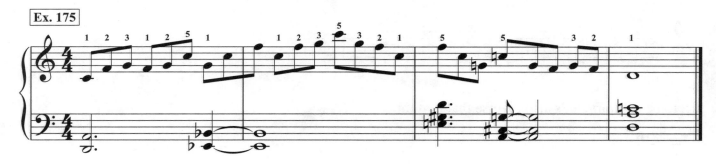

Here's another useful rhythm to learn. It's the same groups of three used in Ex. 175 but each is separated by an 1/8th note rest.

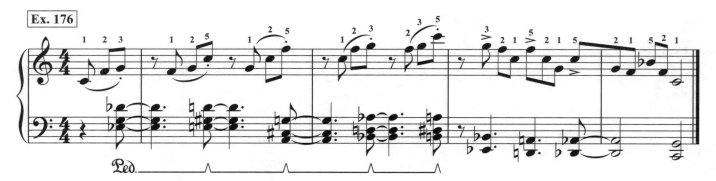

Ex. 177B we break away from the boring, training-wheel rhythms in the previous examples and show that the inversions of our three-note shape can actually be strung together to form a seamless phrase. Before you play it, you might first try Ex. 177A. It's a blocking exercise for the final two measures of 177B. Notice that in those two measures the weight of the hand is centered over the 2nd finger almost constantly.

For those of you who are counting, almost 2/3 of the notes in Ex. 177B are played with just the thumb or index finger. That shows that the physical essence of pentatonic playing is different than the more evenly distributed fingerings involved in traditional European music.

ETUDE #33

Etude 33 is a summary of what we've done with the G fourth stack in this chapter. But I did throw in a few new stacks near the end (built on C, F and Bb) to keep you on your toes! The right hand often looks like just a steady stream of notes but it's really accented groups of threes and fours. Drum it on a tabletop.

Pursuing the drum idea, work up the left hand first and think of all those sustained notes as being played on the cymbal. Then think of the left hand staccato notes as sounding like the dry "pop" of a snare drum hit.

The Drummist

(continued on following page)

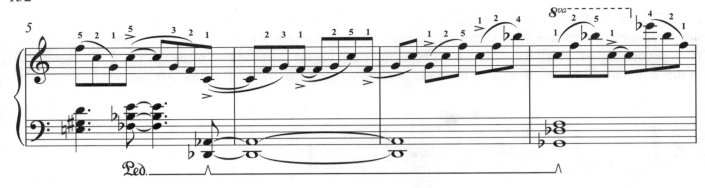

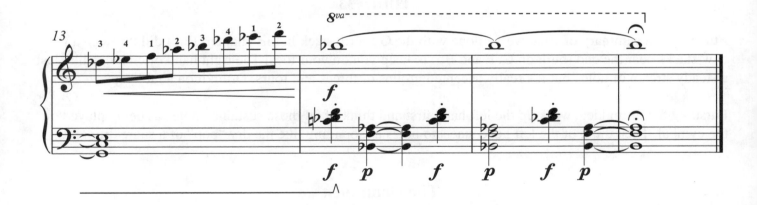

TRANSPOSING CHALLENGES

Since the similarity in feel between all of the white key scales can be confusing, you should go back and transpose Examples 172 and 174-76 to the other all-white scales. It's amazing that the presence of even one black key will make everything feel different. You will have a lot more luck with this if you *practice with your eyes closed*.

CHALLENGE #1:
TRANSPOSING EXERCISE #172

Below are the first couple of measures of Ex. 172 transposed to four different keys (the original was C in minor). Using these as starting points, transpose Ex. 172 to the other all-white keys of D, E, G and A minor as shown below.

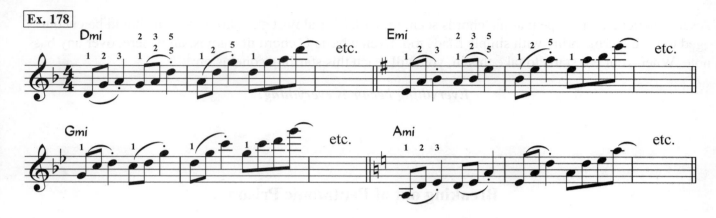

CHALLENGE #2:
TRANSPOSING EXERCISE #175

Now transpose Ex. 175 to the four other all-white keys of D, E, G and A minor as shown below. Keep your thumb in. Good luck and don't hurt yourself!

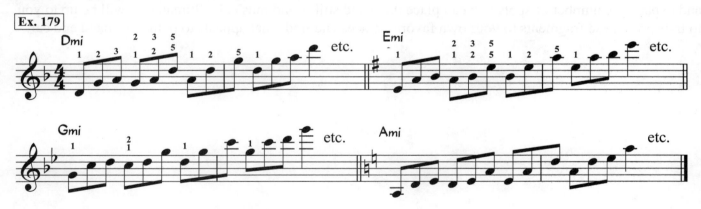

Just to make sure you don't get too comfy in just the white keys, here are the opening notes for exercises 172 and 175 with a starting note of F. The lone black key Bb can really throw the hand off if you're not expecting it!

Before moving on, create your own black key exercises. Go back and play examples 178-79 down a half step. These aren't as scary as they look as long as you keep your thumb in over the keys. No need to get queasy just because you're riding high on the top of the black keys, it's not like they're the Swiss Alps!

Something to Wrap Your Brain Around

After experiencing how pentatonic chords seem to work over almost any harmony, you should be encouraged to try experimenting with simple triads too. Even a basic C chord fits almost anywhere, over any bass note. When your ear starts to take this in, you will reach this startling conclusion:

Everything becomes everything!

Breaking out of Pentatonic Prison

Really? Everything becomes everything?

Right. We'll open that door a crack in the next chapter.

In this chapter we mostly worked with just one stack of perfect fourths and its two inversions. Did you notice how many chords that stack worked well with? In Chapter 31 will begin to move them around a bit and expand the number of spots you can place them and still sound musical. Ultimately it will be up to you to transpose these fragments to your own favorite places and find what appeals to both your hand and ear.

Chapter 31 - The Half-Step Slip

Escaping Pentatonic Prison

You may have noticed that, even though the pentatonic scales can be colored with left hand chords, the absence of any half steps can make them sound bland or similar to New Age music. There are several ways to solve this: *colorful harmony* (which we've already been using), *bending notes* (as discussed back in Chapter 11) and something new that I call the *half-step slip*.

> ### Doing the Slip
> The half-step slip is where a run of pentatonic notes is interrupted by briefly transposing the scale you're working with either up or down a half-step.

For a simple demonstration of that, we'll revisit Etude #2 with a few of the original right-hand notes in measures 3 to 6 transposed up a half-step. The "slip" may startle at first and, to some, maybe sound a bit like fingernails scraping across a blackboard, but it will increase the places your hand can go by a thousand-fold.

Doin' the Slip

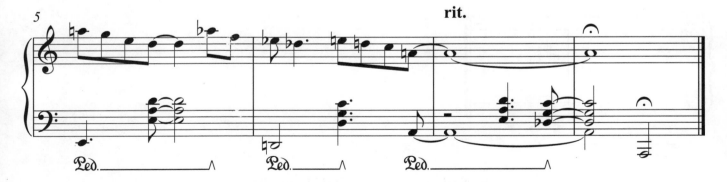

ETUDE #35

In Etude #35, we'll revisit those three-note shapes from Chapter 30 and make music by moving them around a bit. At first glance, the etude may seem like a complex, snaking line but it's actually just arpeggiating the friendly shapes found in the warm-up below - Ex. #181.

After clumping through Ex. 181 for a while, you should be prepared for the fingerings in Etude #35 below. They are not "classical," but are based on quoting from the chord shapes you learned in Ex. 181. Remember, when you are improvising on your own, you will be presumably thinking of music faster can you can invent "perfect" fingerings. As I improvised this etude for this book, I realized that there's no possible way it could have been born without confining myself to moving those chord shapes around with the only fingering my hand "knew." Of course you're free to change things later but the aim here is to show that lines are conceived not one note at a time, but in little bursts of three or four…and don't worry about fingerings, there's no time for that!

Free at Last

Variations Using the Half-Step Slip

Now we'll see how the half-step slip can be used in the context of a 12-bar blues. Example 182 on the following page makes conventional use of some three and four-note chord shapes taken mostly from the C minor pentatonic scale. This example is only a template that will be varied in examples 183 A-B. This is highly rhythmic, so sing or tap out the rhythms until you can't help but hear them.

Ex. 182

Two Variations of Ex. 182

Using the half-step slip is like adding spice to food and should be used sparingly at first. To that end, our first variation of Ex. 182 cautiously moves only a few small groups of notes up a half-step and they're indicated with a small bracket above the notes. These raised notes can cause small shocks similar to a piece of tin foil on a candy bar coming contact with a metal filling. You may want to consult your dentist before proceeding.

Variation #1

Ex. 183A

(continued on following page)

In Ex. 183B I moved the first eight notes up a half-step. Some people may try to analyze them as sharp 9ths or 11ths against a C7 chord but that's not how they're conceived. The "slip" is meant to be a non-intellectual, physical process. The trick for you is to decide how much to use them before it sounds unmusical.

Variation #2

CONSTRUCT-O-MATIC SOLO

Now it's your turn to create some music. Choosing notes shouldn't be too difficult because, hey, we're working with just five-note scales, right? The creative part (and the essence of all music) comes from the rhythms and melodic contours—that is what people mostly "hear" and mistake for notes. Other parts of music are harmony and timbre but those are just add-ons to the real basic stuff.

In example 184 you'll see the rhythms and contours taken from Ex. 182. Take any scale in any key that you have seen in this book and plug them into these rhythms. Try it out on one chord or perhaps a blues or standard tune if that works for you. You'll notice that there are seven three-note shapes implied here plus some four-note shapes. Also try a mirror image of the ups and downs too—ie: start out with a high note and play the first four notes in a downward direction.

> *The lesson here is that if you're operating securely with some coherent rhythms plus a general sense of the direction in which you want your line to flow, you can take more chances with notes. So try some half-step slips now before your hand forgets what they are!*

Ex. 184

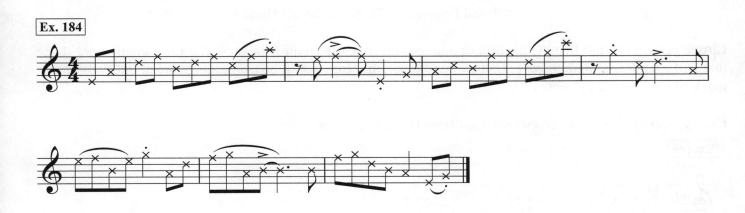

Repeat the same process in Ex. 185. For a real challenge, take the two pick-up notes from the beginning of Ex. 184 above and insert them into the end of the final measure below. Then proceed to play them both non-stop—ie: your newly composed version of Ex. 185 followed by the rhythms in Ex. 184.

Ex. 185

Chapter 32 - Four-Note Shapes

So far, we now have five items in our creative toolbox:
 1) *The half-step slip*
 2) *The 88-note scale (different registers conveying different emotions)*
 3) *Bending notes*
 4) *The concept of using rhythms to generate ideas*
 5) *Using three-note shapes*

In the last two chapters we saw how a single, three-note stack of perfect fourths plus its two inversions could yield all sorts of ideas. In this chapter we will raise the ante by introducing another tool: the *four-note* shape.

Open and Closed Position

There are two basic tactile approaches to using four-note shapes: 1) *closed position* and 2) *open position*.

"Closed Position"—Making a Small Hand

Closed position means that the handful of 4 notes you choose to improvise on will form a small chord shape that will span *less than an octave*. Using closed position means you'll be using lots of small intervals and many of the "next door" notes.

Ex. 186 shows two closed shapes selected from the G minor pentatonic scale.

Ex. 186

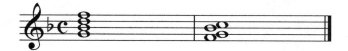

Open Position or Making a "Big Hand"

Open position means that the handful of 4 notes you choose to improvise with will form a larger chord shape that spans an *octave or more*. Since the five scales covered in this book each spans less than an octave, using open position means you're manufacturing large intervals by transposing one of the scale tones either up or down one octave.

Ex. 187 shows two open shapes taken from the G minor pentatonic scale.
 1) The first chord spans a ninth because the D was raised an octave.
 2) The second chord spans only an octave, but it is still considered "open" because the top note is doubling the lower C. Any chord less than an octave in width is considered "closed."

Ex. 187

ETUDE #36

Closed Position

Etude 36 is a blues using four-note groups in *closed position*. In fact, the first 8 measures are composed entirely of just the following two shapes moved about the keyboard:

Example 189 blocks out, in order, all of the shapes found in Etude 36. Note the cool half-step slips in measure three: that's classic Chick Corea stuff. Get this worked up to least 188 beats per minute. Notice that all the chords here use the thumb on the bottom note. *Practice the thumb notes by themselves and always let them guide you to the next chord shape.*

Etude 36 itself involves some fairly advanced bebop but if you spend time working out the blocking process as shown in Ex. 189, your hand will always be over the notes. Ultimately, 17 out of the 21 chords below have the top note played by the weak fifth finger, so you should practice that by itself too.

Every note in the "small hand" Etude 36 comes from one of the four pentatonic scales presented in this book. They appear in groups of 4 to 6 notes in length. Can you identify the groups?

The Great American Pastime

Etude Nº36

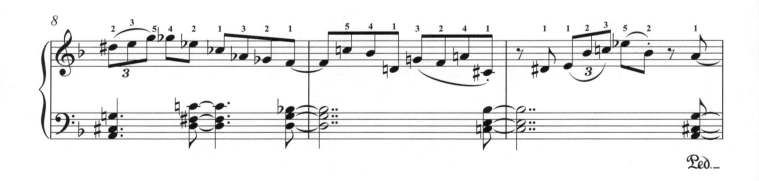

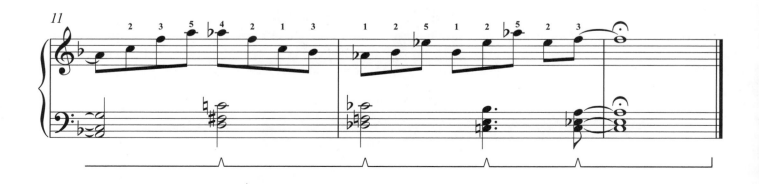

ETUDE #37

Open Position—Making a Big Hand

Etude 37 makes music using four-note shapes in *open position*. Most of the chords span just an octave but Ex. 190 shows a commonly used jazz chord that stretches a 9th. It's the fourth-stack with a major third on top shown in the first measure below. From measure two to the end, that fourth-stack appears six times in succession here, built up from the thumb being on D, F G and finally, D again at the very end. This gives the hand a bit of a stretch and is known as the "So What" chord, which is featured in the famous Miles Davis tune of the same name.

Note that the two chords in the first measure both use the same four notes arranged in open and closed position.

Before you dive into Etude 37, Ex. 191 below gives a preview of how the open position chords in the etude can put pressure on the weak 4th and 5th fingers. Ironically, the solution is not found by strengthening those two fingers but instead, in getting the thumb securely in over the keys on the knuckle.

As soon as you play a chord, instantly release it and move as quickly as possible to the next one. The name of the game is to arrive a millisecond early at your next destination to allow the hand to re-configure for the next chord shape.

Now try playing through Etude 37. At first glance, it appears to be a nightmare of hand stretches and contortions that weave a complex, snaky line. On reflection though, you'll see that it's simply a series of four-note, pentatonic shapes split up into single notes. Nine of the shapes are in open position and five are closed. If this is causes stiffness in your hand, no worries! The etude is followed by two prep exercises (Ex. 192-93) that reveal the secret of making the hand "small" again even playing the larger shapes.

Big Hand, Little Hand

Making the Hand Small Again
Etude 37 was sort of a mean musical joke sprung upon you. The idea was to present huge, awkward intervals and stretches without the benefit of providing the core explanation of how to effectively play them. To play these cool-sounding wide intervals, one needs to perceive and practice them as a series of tiny handfuls. Ex. 192 and 193 on the following page will provide the solution to quieting the hand down.

Ex. 192 on the following page blocks out the first four measures of the "big handed" Etude 37. I temporarily reversed the eighth-note rhythms here so that only the small intervals are emphasized. This creates a series of friendly intervals made of 3rds and 4ths. You should first practice the half-notes by themselves.

Ex. 192

Ex. 193 now returns to accenting the original downbeats of Etude 37 with half-notes. This restores the original "large hand" intervals of 6ths and 7ths. Be aware that the thumb is playing the highest note G on beat three of the third measure. This may feel terrible to the hand at first, but if you loosen up and let go of wherever you are and "think away" to the next pair of notes, I guarantee that you be able to render a graceful and flexible performance of Etude 37.

Ex. 193

Now go back to Etude 37 and see if your hand is quieter and more centered.

ETUDE #38 A

Etude #38A will make equal use of the big and little hand shapes. It is a blues played on the black keys in which the rhythm of the opening four measures is borrowed from Thelonius Monk's famous tune "Straight, No Chaser."

Ex. 194

Etude 38A is a blend of six big-hand shapes and six of the smaller ones. It may seem intimidating or even beyond your abilities at first but it is followed by the two prep exercises 195-196 that reduce it down to a series of "small hand" movements.   The title "Talking Drums" came to me when I realized that the black keys and various rhythms used in Etude 38 resembles those heard on the five-note, African Kalimba or thumb piano. (Don't ask me why I didn't name it "Talking Kalimbas.")

Talking Drums

Prep Exercises for Etude 38A

Ex. 195 is an inventory of notes from the first few measures of Etude 38. Notice how in the first three measures that the thumb moves all over the place but the 3rd, 4th and 5th fingers remain immobile. That acts as an anchor for the hand. Notice also, in measures 3-5, that the situation is reversed and the thumb has it's turn to remain immobile and rest of the fingers now move all over the place.

Ex. 196 blocks out the downbeats for the first half of the etude. You will have to keep shifting the weight to the right and the left side of the hand to accommodate the half notes.

TRANSPOSING CHALLENGE

On the following page we'll transpose Etude 38 up a half step to the all-white key of E minor. After the misery of all the black keys you just wrestled with, this white key experience should be a piece of cake! Or is it? The right hand part will work well over a C Major 7th chord too. Keep in mind that the rhythms are based on Monk's "Straight, No Chaser." Try your own pentatonic ideas using those rhythms.

168

Talking Drums II

Ex. 197 is a blocking exercise for Etude 38B.

> *"Ahem. . .and in conclusion"*
> *Now that you've experienced a taste of conceiving notes in groups of threes and fours, you may have a feeling that "the big hand" shapes are, literally, a bit of a stretch for you. But in the end, I would wager that your hands will now open up a bit, playing fewer small groups of convenient, "next door" notes and will begin cooking up ideas that are conceived in octave-wide handfuls.*

Part IX: Slash Chords vs. Linear Improvising

"This is the stuff that makes us play and sound smarter than we really are."

Chapter 33 - Chordal vs. Linear Improvising

BEYOND BRILLIANT

> *This is the stuff that makes us play and sound smarter than we really are.*
>
> *This is the opulent stuff we dream about playing but wake up the next morning to find that we can't recall a single note of it.*
>
> *This is the "outside" stuff you wildly grab for, quickly run out of gas in about eight measures and then return to the old, sorry way you were trying to escape from in the first place.*

We've been stressing how the amount of rote materials and knowledge you have in your hands greatly influence your creativity (it really is a case of matter over mind.) This chapter will take a look at another way to use your physical interaction with the keys to shape the very character of what you play.

Up to this point, we have only discussed linear ideas. That is to say, we've used the right hand to create single-note strings that make some kind of musical sense. Now it's time to take a look at *vertical* or *chord-based* improvising. This means before you choose one of the scales in this book to apply to a given chord, you might want to evaluate your choice in a different way. i.e., just thinking that a "C major chord = C major scale" is fairly primitive and dead ends pretty quickly.

Here's how you go about doing something like this:

To improvise on any chord larger than a triad, you need to extract the essential sound of that larger chord. That is done via a smaller three-note chord. This simpler, smaller chord will appear to be "outside" the original but will actually be a logical extension of it. If you can identify this extension chord (no pun), then you are armed with a powerful tool: something easy to play on that is also a clear, lucid way to layer all the cool color-tones onto complex chords.

First we need do is a little review of basic harmony. Before you snort your milk out of your nose at that thought, be advised that this basic stuff will not remain that way for long.

Quartal vs. Tertian Harmony

So far, this book has spent a lot of time on harmony based on fourths, otherwise known as *quartal harmony*. That's because the subject at hand has been the pentatonic scale, which is a stack of fourths rearranged into a scale pattern. Now we will look at harmony built in thirds. That's the most common, everyday stuff that's been used over the past three centuries from Bach to rock. Harmony built up in stacks of thirds is called *tertian harmony*.

> ### *Tertian Harmony*
>
> *The basic unit of tertian harmony is the triad (shown in Ex. 198a below).*
>
> *If a triad doesn't sound thick enough, rich enough or as opulent as you'd like, then you merely add another third to the stack and you're in the realm of seventh chords (Ex. 198b).*
>
> *If you want your jazz playing to sound any more modern than say, 1945, then you raise the ante once again by adding yet another third and you get a ninth chord (Ex. 198c).*
>
> *If you add just two more thirds to the stack, you're done! You've just taken all the seven "white notes" of the C major scale and reordered them into a big pile of thirds (Ex. 198d below). Yes, I know, that huge stack sounds terrible when you play it as written but we'll thin it out for you here shortly. For now, we'll go as high as the ninth.*
>
> Ex. 198
>
>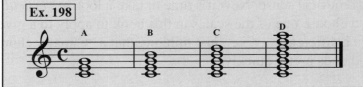

And Now For the Interesting Stuff

If a plain C major scale is the raw material that simultaneously expresses a C triad, a C major 7th chord and a C major 9th chord (as shown above) then how do you go about playing those notes in a manner that will convince the listener of which chord you mean to convey?

The simple answer: *build a model (stacked in thirds) of whatever chord you're playing on. Then choose the highest three notes and throw away everything below that! That is known as the slash chord method.*

For a fuller view of how this thinning out process is accomplished, Chapter 34 will look at how the slash chord concept can be used with seventh chords.

Chapter 34 - Slash Chords and Sevenths

We'll begin slash chords by using C major 7th as an example. First, extract the top three notes to give you something to work with: those notes will spell out an E minor chord.

Now all you have to do is just play the basic C chord in the left hand then place your right hand over an E minor pentatonic and play away! Do not think "C major," think E minor! Forget C major. Just let your left hand play that chord.

ETUDE #39

Etude 39 shows how to do this. The first two measures are C major 7th but the right hand is expressing E minor via the E minor pentatonic scale. In measures 3 and 4 we've moved on to an F major 7th chord where the right hand is expressing A minor via the A minor pentatonic scale over the F chord. Then it returns to C major 7th again in line two of the music.

Fancy

If you think about it, even though Etude 39 above is a series of C and F chords, the quickest and most colorful way to express them is to ignore that fact and play on E minor and A minor instead. These major 7ths can sound pretty bland, so by choosing the darker sounding minor pentatonics to play on, at least you can get enough of a bluesy feeling to rescue the situation!

This is just another example of the "Escaping Major 7th Hell" concept briefly discussed earlier. You may recall that's where you can use minor or a blues scales to enrich the major 7th chords (see Etude #8.)

Slash Chords

Now that you've had some small bit of experience with the concept of focusing on another chord outside the root chord, you need to be aware that there is actually a system of labeling used to communicate this approach. It involves a small chord formula split into two halves that can greatly simplify the most complex chord symbols. This is the origin of the term *slash chords*.

In Etude 39 above, we dealt with the C and F major 7th harmonies by playing on an E minor and an A minor chord. In slash chord notation, those would be written as **Emi/C** and **Ami/F**. The first term on the *left* side names the *right-hand chord*. The term on the *right* side names the *left-hand bass note*. If that seems awkward, just understand that originally they were aligned vertically back in the day when music was more casually written-out by hand for jam sessions. You can see in these two examples how the low bass notes, C and F, clearly occupy the lower half in the older style of slash chord notation.

$$\frac{\text{Emi}}{\text{C}} \qquad \frac{\text{Ami}}{\text{F}}$$

Chapter 35 - Slash Chords and Ninths

This chapter will explore three different ninth chords: the dominant ninth, the major ninth and the minor ninth with a raised seventh. Each chord has a distinct flavor that will be demonstrated by having a single etude harmonized into three different versions.

Keep in mind that the common thread running all through this section of the book is: *build a model of whatever chord you're playing on, choose the highest three notes to build a simple chord and throw away everything below that!*

The Dominant-Ninth Chord

We create a dominant-ninth chord by extending our basic C7th chord up a third by adding a D on top. Remember that a dominant-seventh is the one with the lowered 7th, located two half-steps below the octave.

Ex. 201 is a little reminder that the Coltrane b7th pentatonic scale (see Chapter 20) is just a compressed version of the five notes found in the ninth chord above.

The next step towards improvising on a C9th chord is to select either a) the top three notes or b) the top four notes as shown in Ex. 202. Your choice.

Written as slash chords, C9 could be Gmi/C or Emi7 (b5) /C. Either way, your hand has a different "grab" other than the root position C chord with which to plink out ideas. Basically what you do is put your right hand over a G minor chord. That way, the hand will feed the brain as much as the other way around.

Examples 203 and 204 will now apply the same thinning-out process to both the F9th and F#9th chord stacks. All these chords will be used Etude 40A.

176

In Ex. 203 F9th can be seen as Cmi/F or Ami7 (b5)/F:

In Ex. 204 the F#9th can be approached as C#mi/F# or A#mi7 (b5)/F#:

Ex. 205 lets you test-drive some two-handed voicings for the ninth chord. It begins with the distilled, three-note version and then finishes out with the slightly more opulent, four-note version.

ETUDE #40A

Etude #40A on the following page now takes the three ninth-chord stacks shown in examples 202-205 and makes music with them. There are only about 5 notes in this etude that are not quoted directly from those stacks. You'll find that your hand spends most its time over G and C minor chords.

That burst of "odd" notes in measure six comes from using an F#9th chord. A basic F#7th chord is nearly indistinguishable from a C7th (they share the same 3rd and 7th) so I used both those chords in the left hand to muddy the waters a bit.

Custer's First Stand

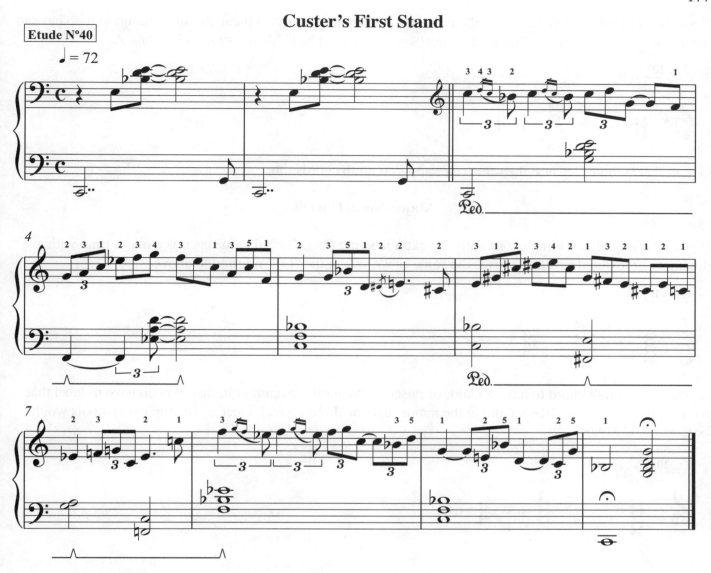

We're now ready to move on and begin looking at some other ninth chords. Before we do that, a little explanation of chord terminology might be in order here.

Chord Symbols and Terminology

When there is a major triad involved, you don't ever have to ever label it as such…it's a given. Just plain old "C" means a C major chord, no matter how many 9ths or 11ths or 13ths you may see written above it.

But if there is a seventh present in a chord you do have to label that. This is where it gets tricky. In this case, if you do not qualify the seventh with any extra labeling or descriptors (for instance, the chord symbol "G7") that means it is a dominant or lowered seventh chord. That's the seventh that resides two half-steps below the octave.

If you want the seventh to be "natural" or "raised" or "major " (they all mean the same thing) you do have to label that with a qualifier. In that case, typical symbols would be C Maj7...or C M7... or CΔ.

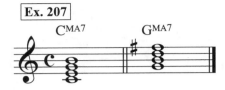

Got all that? Good. Because the same rules apply to ninth chords too.

Major-Ninth Chords

If you *do not* qualify a ninth chord with any extra labeling (ie: "G9") that means it is a major triad with a dominant or lowered seventh. This is the same as we saw in the "G7" referred to above.

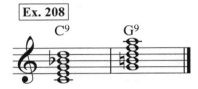

If you want a ninth chord to have a major or raised or "natural" seventh in it, then you do have to label that with a qualifier (exactly like we did in the major seventh chord above). Once again, typical symbols would be C Maj9, C M9 or CΔ9.

ETUDE #40B

Etude 40B on the following page is basically the same as 40A except that the flatted thirds and sevenths (the E and B flats) have been raised to become E and B naturals. In other words, all the dominant ninths (with the flatted 7ths) have been replaced with major ninths (with natural 7ths) and the piece is instantly recast with airiness and serenity prevailing. The stage lights have been switched from a blue, nocturnal shade to a brighter, midday glow. Or maybe not. Describing music with colors probably says more about me than the music...ha! But you get the idea. Major ninths speak a totally different message than dominant ninths.

In any case, pretty much the same slash chords described back in Chapter 34 will apply: G major or E minor triads will be used over the C major 7th chords and C major or A minor triads will be used over the F major 7th chords.

Major Leagues

Minor Ninth Chords with a Raised Seventh

The minor ninth chord with the raised seventh has an interesting sound. With its lowered third and natural 7th it combines elements of both the minor triad and major seventh chords.

This major/minor conflict exudes a 1950s era film *noir* vibe and has been used in countless private detective and spy films ranging from James Bond to the old Humphrey Bogart and Sidney Greenstreet black and white classics.

Ex. 210 shows two of these chords as used in Etude 40C. They're framed in the context of the key of C minor. Notice how the switch from the C minor to the F minor chord below introduces an E natural into the equation, creating that kind of haunting major/minor sound that is so typical of minor chords with a raised 7th.

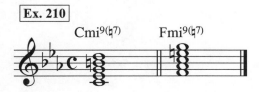

ETUDE #40C

With exception of measure six, Etude 40C is made up entirely from the two minor chords shown above. *The measures with C minor chords use the G major b6th pentatonic scale to express them. In a similar manner, the measures with the F minor chords use the C major b6th pentatonic scale to express them.*

Think about those last italicized sentences for a minute. What is the relationship of each minor chord and the particular b6th scale that expresses it? Then we'll explore that idea in the next chapter after you had a chance to get acquainted with Etude 40C below.

H. Bogart

Chapter 36 - Two New "Rules"

Two Killer Aps for the Flat 6th Pentatonic

Before moving on to Etude 41, it's time to pause, clarify and summarize two of ways that the major (b6th) pentatonic scale has been applied over and over in this book.

The first item refers to the idea stated way back on page 147 (Ex. 134) that *"Measures with C minor chords can use the G major (b6th) pentatonic scale to express C minor."*

How does that work?

Well, it's very easy. Simply take a G major (b6th) pentatonic scale and try, as best as you can, to arrange it into a stack of thirds as shown below.

Well, how about that? In Ex. 211B the scale easily rearranges into an outline of a C minor 9th with a natural 7th. In fact, the G major (b6th) scale makes up 5/7 of the complete C minor stack as shown in Ex. 211C above.

Here's the same process applied to an F minor chord. In this instance, take the C major b6th pentatonic scale and arrange it into a stack of thirds. Presto! That C major scale unfolds into an extended F minor chord.

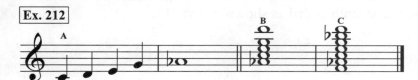

RULE #1

OK, so now we can deduce a little rule for minor chords: *to play on a minor chord with a raised seventh. select a major (b6th) pentatonic scale whose root is a perfect 5th above or a perfect fourth below the minor chord. For example, you would use an F(b6th) scale to play on a Bb minor chord.*

This "rule" is plainly apparent in the opening five measures of the short excerpt from Etude 41 on the next page. Measure one and also four and five are a G (b6th) scale over a C minor chord. Measure 2 is a C (b6th) over an F minor. Only the third measure features a different scale. More on that shortly.

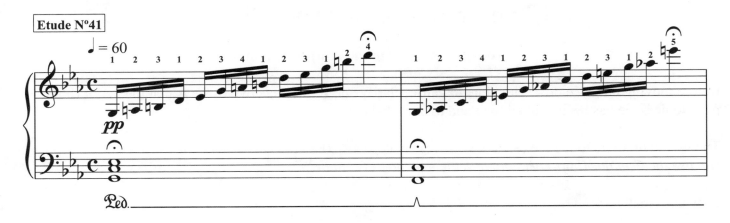

So what's up with that chord and scale in measure three above? Basically, it's a G7 with a raised 5th. Or to put it another way, it's a G augmented triad with a seventh added as shown in Ex. 213.

That raised fifth (D# or Eb) happens to be the minor third from the key of C minor, which is the prevailing key of Etude 41. Altering that note just adds a bit of C minor coloration to the G chord.

OK. So, what five-note scale best expresses the particular flavor of the G7 chord? You guessed it: the major, (b6th) pentatonic again comes to the rescue! In the case of this G augmented 7th harmony, you would use an E flat major, b6th scale to express it. Just for your reference, since that Eb scale begins two steps below the G it would be the flatted sixth of the chord.

How in the world does that Eb pentatonic relate to a G7th chord? Check out Ex. 214 as we unfold and reorder the scale tones into a huge chord.

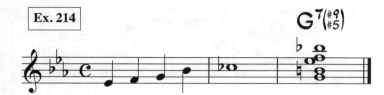

Wow! The Eb b6th pentatonic scale actually is the G+7 chord!

Just for fun, here are some cool, two-handed G+7 chords from those five notes.

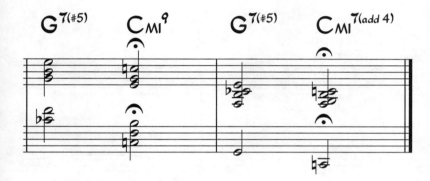

RULE #2

OK, so now we can deduce a little rule for dominant 7th chords: *to play on a dominant chord with a raised fifth. select a major (b6th) pentatonic scale that is a major third below the dominant chord. For example, use an F(b6th) scale to play over an A7 chord.*

We'll finish off this section on ninth chords by putting it all together in Etude 41 on the following pages. Virtually every measure is based around Rules #1 and #2 discussed above. For instance, the C and F minor chords in measures one and two below employ Rule #1. In the third measure, the G aug.7th chord implied there follows Rule #2.

ETUDE 41
The Hanging Garden

C minor   F minor

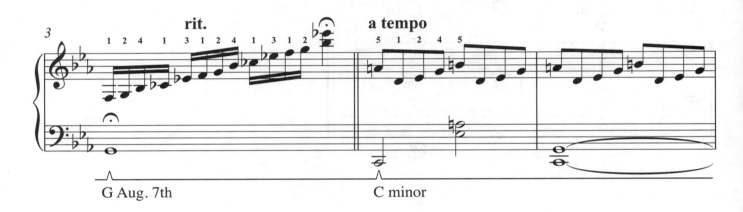

G Aug. 7th   C minor

Chapter 37 - Pentatonic Block Chord Soloing

To make linear ideas work well as music, all one has to have is a decent sense of melody. Melody itself is a process similar to stringing pearls together: each note is a "pearl" that needs to be chosen and placed so that its color and size (duration) contributes to a pleasing, organic whole. But in chordal improvising, "melody" takes on a different meaning. We'll show how that if you play fistfuls of chords in a rhythmically coherent manner, the "melody" that results is not important. In other words, when you play cool-sounding chords one after another, there will be an accidental melody present (the highest pitch) by virtue of some note being the top one on the stack, but that's not very important. What is important is:

A) that each chord should be made up from the intervals found in a given pentatonic scale and chosen for its "color," even if that choice occasionally "violates" basic rules of theory. The half-step slip really becomes useful here.

B) that the force that drives you to play a string of chords is mainly rhythmic in nature. In other words, you suddenly need to become a drummer.

The best way to get started is to arbitrarily choose a little chord algorithm to work with. A 1-3-5 chord stack on the black keys will do nicely. "1-3-5" in this case means place your right hand over any five black keys in a row but only press down your 1st, 3rd and 5th fingers. Play through Ex. 216A and you find that walking this handful up the black keys yields three 4th stacks plus one major and one minor triad. Instead of 1-3-5, you could also choose any other note combination that you like, ie: 2, 3, 4 or 1, 4, 5, etc.

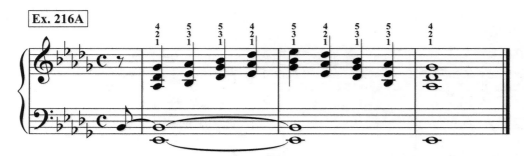

In example 216B we cheat a little bit. We uniformly harmonize all five black keys with pure 4th stacks. This violates the black key pentatonic scale a bit by adding one white key but it makes the terrain a little more predictable for the hand and this easier to play. The choice is yours as to which one you like best.

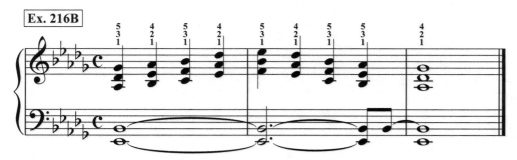

First Inversion Fourth Stack

Ex. 217A presents the black-key chords from Ex. 216A in first inversion. This yields a new sound with lots of "pinched" sounding intervals a major-second apart. Note that there is both a Gb major and an Eb minor chord present in the mix that warm things up a bit.

Ex. 217B is the first inversion of the pure fourth stacks from Ex. 216B. This yields a tighter sound with no triads to warm up all those major-second intervals.

Second Inversion Fourth Stack

The next step is to learn the *second inversions* of the all-black key stacks from Ex. 216A

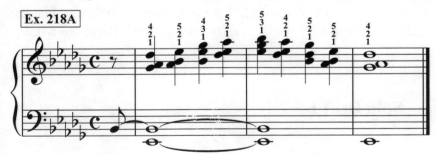

We finish the series with the second-inversion shapes of the pure fourth stacks from Ex. 216B, the one that contained all pure 4th stacks.

Even with just the basic chords in Ex. 216A and B plus their two inversions, you've already harmonized the entire pentatonic scale several times over. Some melody notes are getting four and even five different chords to color them. Bb is the winner because it is present in the most stacks, which means that there are five chord choices available to play underneath it. Bear in mind that my choice to use the 1-3-5 chord shape as a demonstration model was totally arbitrary on my part. You could also run this process with the Coltrane pentatonic or the Major b6th scale and get stunning results!

Ex. 219 summarizes everything we just did with the 1-3-5 chord shape by showing the five black-key pentatonic melody notes (plus an F) with all the chords available to harmonize them. Even this cautious, conservative process has yielded 20 different chords to color six melody notes.

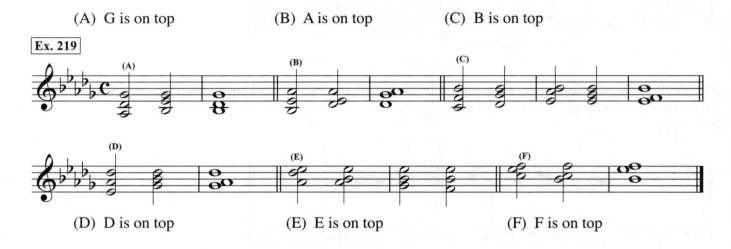

(A) G is on top   (B) A is on top   (C) B is on top

(D) D is on top   (E) E is on top   (F) F is on top

ETUDE #42A

Etude 42A now makes use of the block chords summarized above. And remember—the force that drives you to play these strings of chords is mainly rhythmic in nature. In other words, there's not much of a melody here. This kind of music making comes from the rhythms and coloration that the harmonies provide. Just try playing the melody notes (the top note) of each chord below by itself…pretty boring, huh? There are a few half-step slips to add variety.

Spin Drift I

(continued on following page)

Chapter 38 - White Key Pentatonic Chords

Now we'll take those black key chords (or "black pearls" as they were referred to in Chapter 37) and change them into "white pearls."

To accomplish this, we'll transpose the various Eb minor chords from Chapter 37 down a half step to D minor. Exercises 220-221 present an abbreviated review of them. Once again, note that the chords in the first three measures of Ex. 220 are strictly limited to the five notes from the D minor pentatonic scale but the next three measures (after the double bar line) are pure fourth stacks. This adds the extra note " B" to the mix.

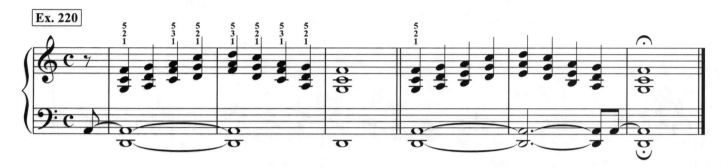

Ex 221 contains the first and second inversions of the chords above.

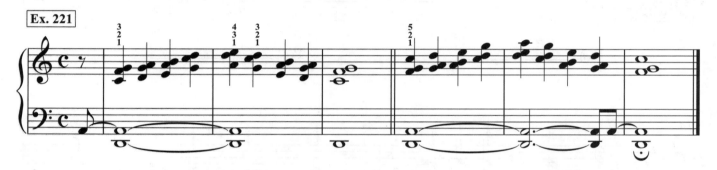

ETUDE #42B

Etude 42B gives a sense of how much music might be made on just the white keys if you're constantly recoloring the "melody notes" with different harmonies. The exceptions are the half-step slips that throw in some black keys in line two. Oddly enough, I find these acres of all-white keys more difficult to play than the black ones.

Spin Drift II

Chapter 39 - Two-Handed Chords

There is a fascinating array of cool, two-handed chords that are made up (or mostly made up) from the notes in the pentatonic scale. The perfect fourth intervals contained in them generally sound more modern to our ears today than the earlier 1940s and 50s bebop harmonies which are based on thirds. These fourth-based, pentatonic chords can "speak" many music languages from the 1970's to today, including modal jazz, Latin, free jazz, fusion music, country music and modern classical. In the jazz world, pianists McCoy Tyner and Chick Corea have been the reigning masters of pentatonic chords since the 1960s.

Example 222 shows one of the most basic and well-known pentatonic chords in jazz history, which was introduced by Miles Davis on his 1958 album "Kind of Blue." The two-chord sequence below is the basis of his famous tune "So What."

There are two ways to hear and feel these chords. One is to perceive them as simple *major triads* in the right hand with a couple of color tones added in the left. Example 222 shows a G and an F major triad with stems up and the two pairs color tones with the stems down. Are these chords coloring the key of G? Or is it really expressing D minor?...or is it really A minor? The answer really is "all of the above." Try playing those bass notes under the chords and you'll hear for yourself.

.The other way to visualize the chords is to see them as stacks of fourths with a major third perched on top as an afterthought. I think this is closer to the essence of the sound of these chords while Ex. 222 above seems more like a fingering diagram to show how to conveniently divide the notes between two hands.

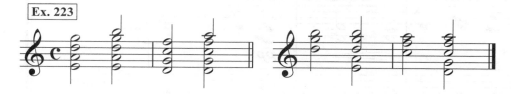

ETUDE #43

Etude 43 runs the "So What" chords from above through five different minor keys.

The Door

(continued on following page)

Now that you've experienced the basic shape of the "So What" chord we'll go ahead and leverage that fist-ful of notes into something much broader. Example 224 begins the process by walking the chords up the white keys, starting on D as the top note. *Only three of these seven chords are the same as the original "So What" chord but the uniformity of the white keys won't communicate this fact to your hands.* The remaining four chords are all slightly different animals, which will become painfully evident when we move off the white keys in a moment. For now, here is the white key version. On what three beats does the original "So What" shape appear?

194

Ex. 224 B transposes everything down one step to C minor. Now you can feel what it's really like to negotiate its way through the different chord shapes.

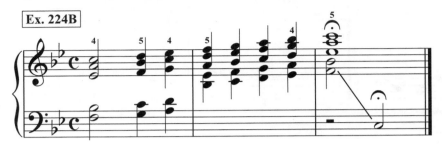

And now for the varsity version, Ex 224 C will move to the black key hell of E flat minor.

The Fourth-Stack Walk

We'll now leave the "So What" chord voicing and move on to walking through the fourth-stack shapes in D minor. As you begin with D as the top note and begin to walk down the white keys you'll notice how many perfect fourths have now become tritones (augmented fourths.) Only three of the seven chords contain all perfect fourths. On what three steps do they occur? Again, the fingers won't "feel" the differences in the various chord types here but they certainly will as soon as you start adding black keys.

C Minor.

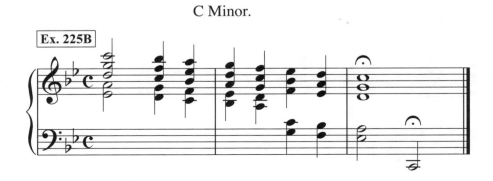

Eb minor.

Chord Anatomy

Now that Ex. 225A, B, and C have presented the "fourth stack walk" in three different keys, your hand has no doubt figured out that only three of the seven chords are all pure fourths. But what about the other four chords? How many different chords are among them? Or all they all the same? Figuring out each chord is the key to quickly and accurately transposing them.

Chapter 40 - Third and Fourth Stacks, Call and Response

ETUDE #44

Etude 44 will be the last of the chord-oriented pieces in this book and will sum up all of the minor penta-tonic harmonies presented so far (plus a couple of other little surprises too). There is, however, one final piece of business before jumping into this etude. This involves looking at the series of chords found in the eight-measure introduction of Etude 44. Here are the opening two measures of an A+7:

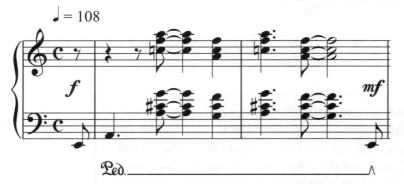

These chords are derived from the F major (b6th) pentatonic scale, which, as you may recall, contains the tritone interval G-Db (or G-C#.) This enables the scale to wander from chord to chord and fit perfectly in many situations such as Eb7, A7 and B minor chords. But how did we arrive at getting the exact chords shown above? Well, there are actually two basic ways to get chords like these.

The F major (b6th) Scale and Dominant 7th Chords

The first way is to view this flat 6th scale is as an F triad combined with the tritone C# to G (shown in Ex. 226 B.) Since that tritone is the heart of an A7 chord, it's possible lower it one octave and have it be the color harmony for an A7 triad as shown below in measure four. Two inversions follow in measure 5.

Even though there is no bass note "A" to fill out the sound in measures 4-5 above, you still wind up with a beautiful, altered A7 chord voicing. Today we would label that complex chord as an F triad over an A7 chord or simply F/A7. That's 100 times simpler than the old way of labeling it as A+7 (#9) plus it gives you two simple handholds two work with (and jam on too!)

The same poly-chord idea also applies to the D minor chord in the last measure of Ex. 226. Calling it E minor over a D minor 6th is clear and elegant. But back in day, 1950s beboppers might have called that one D mi6/9 (11). That's a pretty cool looking algorithm for sure, but a bit confusing!

The second way to draw a cool chord out of the F major(b6th) scale is to think of it as an open fifth interval of F and C over the remaining three notes G, A and C#. If you reshuffle the order of those last three a bit, they spell out an A7 with the 5th (E) missing. Then you can lower those notes down an octave and put 'em in the bass clef as shown in Ex. 227 B.

The three chords above labeled *F/A7 or A7(#9)* all have the same notes. They're just re-fingered to prevent the hands overlapping and the bass note A is moved down an octave. I love that final A triad over the D minor 6th chord! To my ears it sounds as cool as the crazy Dmi 6th at the end of Ex 226.

Even if the entire process outlined in 227 only leads you to keep that particular A7(#9) chord in your arsenal, it's well worth it. Transpose the final two A7 to D minor chords in Ex. 226-227 into all 12 keys and you'll really have gotten something from the lowly major-flat 6th scale. You'll be ready to do film scores!

All ten all of the chords in the eight-measure introduction of Etude 44 below are drawn from the ones discussed above. They stand out because they are based on stacks of thirds whereas most of the chords in the rest of etude are made up of various fourth stacks. Speaking of which, here is a final Etude 44 warm up focusing on the single sequence of fourth stacks in measures 13-14 which are inconveniently interrupted by the pesky black key, Bb.

ETUDE #44   (Summertime Variations)

Etude 44 is a variation based on George Gershwin's "Summertime" and is organized into little call and response patterns. The eight-measure introduction is a sort of shouting "Gather around me, I have a story to tell" attention-getter, which then subsides at the end to allow the "tale" to begin quietly in measure nine.

The first statement in our "tale" (shown in Ex 229) opens with three right-hand notes doing the "call." That is followed by the "response" done with the huge chords.

198

Another call and response pattern begins immediately as shown in Ex. 230 below. The best way to define these is to play the "call" fairly loudly and then make the response quieter, as if it were an echo. The alternating patterns should resemble a church preacher shouting out a phrase and then being answered by the congregation or perhaps a blues singer singing a phrase in a nightclub and then being answered or encouraged by the audience.

Summertime Variations

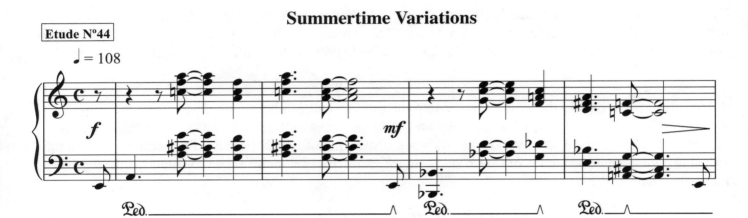

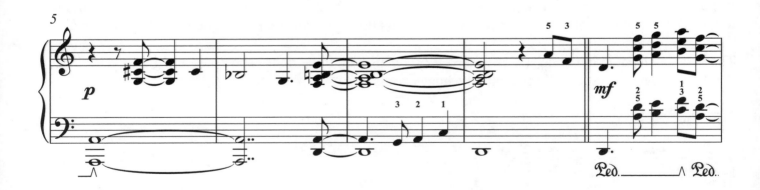

(continued on following page)

(continued on following page)

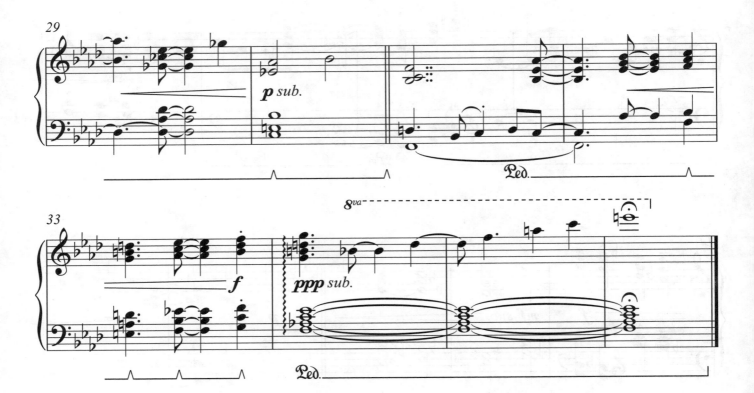

Chapter 41 - Two Handed Chord-Drumming

ETUDE #45

The last two chapters were all about moving two-fisted chords around the keyboard, which is one of most powerful sounds available to a pianist. Now we'll look at an exciting variation, that of using alternating hands like a drummer.

Etude 45 begins with sparse, single-note single note textures before expanding into fuller chords. Ex. 231 is a table-top drumming exercise that allows you to practice the rhythms of the first four measures of Etude 45 before you have to deal with the notes.

"R" means pat with the right hand and "L" refers to the left hand. Notice that the left hand plays almost exclusively on the 2nd and 4th beats only!

Here are the notes that go with the rhythms above. Notice that the only accents are in the right hand on the fourth beats. The left hand notes are in the treble clef and those with a parenthesis ( ) are to be "ghosted" or played with almost no volume.

Ex. 233-234 are taken from the middle of Etude 45 where the chords get thicker.

Here are the notes that go with the rhythms in Ex. 233. They start at rehearsal letter B section of Etude 45. Beware of the change of clef in the left hand.

ETUDE #45

Bach's Lunch

Part X: Coda

These pieces are a summation, a final musical feast or smorgasborg created from the five scales we've examined in this book. I had originally intended to title them "Prelude and Lude" but, in the end, I figured that might be a bit "too hip for the room!" Enjoy!

Chapter 42 - Prelude and Fugue

Here is a jazz prelude followed by a fugue that will serve as a kind of summing up of many things discussed in this volume. The prelude is a slow blues and you can see it performed here:
http://www.youtube.com/watch?v=rCD8nfJhQsA

Prelude 1

Marius Nordal

210

Fugue I

A fugue is a process piece with 3 to 4 independent lines of melody where a simple theme (called the "subject") is layered upon itself. In this fugue the subject enters three times: in measures one, seven and ten (in the bass clef.) You can see a performance of it here: https://www.youtube.com/watch?v=2MUC5JMIb10

©2011 Marius Nordal

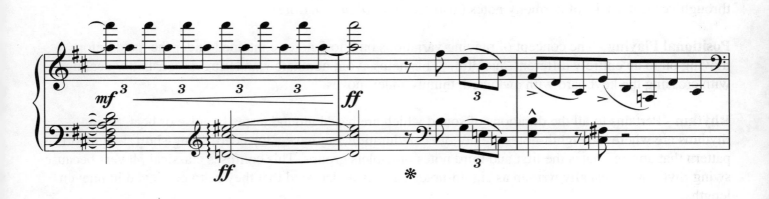

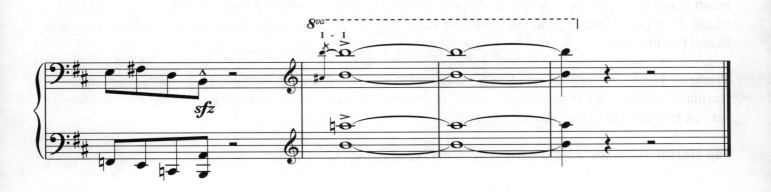

Glossary

88 Note Scale - The view that every note has a different personality that keeps changing as you move all the way up the keyboard. This idea contradicts the traditional notion of having only 12 different note names which can mislead one into believing that each octave is essentially the same. The concept of 88 unique notes should encourage one to play in all registers and avoid the rut of only using the middle of the piano.

Bending Notes - Starting at a lower pitch and then gliding or "bending" it upwards to the "correct" pitch. Bending also includes starting high and then gliding downwards too.

Etude - A piece of music composed for the purpose of solving a specific technical problem.

Fourth Stack - A chord consisting of notes separated by perfect fourths.

Half-Step Slip - Briefly transposing a chord or a musical idea up or down a half tone from where the ear would normally expect to hear it.

Hand Shapes - Quoting small groups of three to four single melody notes taken from conventional or unconventional chord shapes. This opens up the concept of thinking in terms of several notes at a time.

Inversion - Changing the sound of a chord by removing the bottom note and placing it on the top. This allows a new note to become the bass tone.

Linear Improvising - The concept of improvising melodies without being unduly concerned about whether the notes you're choosing to play match the ones in the chordal accompaniment. In other words, it involves thinking in a linear, melodic manner "across the page" rather than thinking literally "down" the page through vertical stacks of harmony notes (also see *vertical improvising*).

Positional Playing - The concept of playing variations on 3 to 5 notes contained under the hand before moving on to an entirely different "handful." This helps avoid nomadic wandering or constantly dealing with crossing the keyboard with awkward, thumb-under moves.

Rhythm - Pertains to all the durations of sound which are based around a steady pulse or beat. Swing rhythms are where the eighth-notes are not of even duration, but have a lopsided, "long-short, long-short" pattern that approximates the first and third notes of triplets groups. This confuses classical players because swing rhythms are usually written as eighth-notes but it is understood that they're to be played in uneven lengths.

Slash Chords - A process where you simplify a complex chord symbol by first deleting the root and then taking the highest 3 notes from the top of the stack to spell another simple chord. For example, a G11 chord would become F/G.

Timbre - The characteristic sound or "tone color" of any instrument. A flute might sound "silvery" or "brilliant" and an oboe might sound "nasal" or "reedy." Because of its wide range, a piano can simulate various timbres and percussion instruments.

Top Harmony - Adding a harmony note or notes above the melodic line.

Transpose - The act of shifting a melody or chords up or down to another key.

Tritone - An interval that is three whole-steps wide and divides an octave in half. Dominant 7th chords with roots a tritone apart sound very similar because their 3rd and 7th degrees (themselves a tritone in width) are interchangeable. For instance, G7th and Db7th are often substituted for one another in jazz and pop music.

Vertical Improvising - The concept of improvising melodies whose notes are largely selected from the ones in the chordal accompaniment. This involves thinking literally "down" the page through vertical stacks of the inventory of harmony notes being played at that moment (also see *linear improvising*).

Voicing - The art of rearranging the notes in a chord to achieve a desired sound or resonance. This is accomplished by altering, adding, doubling and deleting selected notes.

Selected Video Lessons From YouTube

Bending Notes	http://www.youtube.com/watch?v=P_lLPAivsZU
Blues Scale	http://www.youtube.com/watch?v=ReJHeMZY9k8
Coltrane Pentatonic	http://www.youtube.com/watch?v=yuZzqXgZpao
Creativity-Rhythms	http://www.youtube.com/watch?v=oukrKemes4o
Diminished Scale	http://www.youtube.com/watch?v=LJQIfjlw24Q
How to Play Fast	http://www.youtube.com/watch?v=aKVLXDS4De0
Jazz Modes Explained	http://www.youtube.com/watch?v=BCmfM9lcRZg
Major 7th Hell	http://www.youtube.com/watch?v=hNW5KdWjlsQ
Minor Pentatonics	http://www.youtube.com/watch?v=CbaK2FjPSWw
Play Genius Jazz	http://www.youtube.com/watch?v=fAzwviIwoU
What Instrument is a piano?	http://www.youtube.com/watch?v=yLwykalX2KQ

Selected Performances From You Tube

Cherokee	http://www.youtube.com/watch?v=SpXssOw8Pq0
Good Vibrations	http://www.youtube.com/watch?v=4puRer00Epg
Molokini Reef	http://www.youtube.com/watch?v=TAESB9kSUtk
Notoriety Blues	http://www.youtube.com/watch?v=Zn-JVEi4uAY
Over The Rainbow	http://www.youtube.com/watch?v=Zn-JVEi4uAY
School Days	http://www.youtube.com/watch?v=qbAwox-uAmM
Si Ti Vois Ma Mere	http://www.youtube.com/watch?v=EiKj-8Z9v3k
White Christmas	http://www.youtube.com/watch?v=66DTtXUV6r4

CDs on the Origin Label by Marius Nordal

"Ways of the Hand"	Origin 82383
"Notoriety"	Origin 82361
"Boomer Jazz"	Origin 82545

For more information, visit: Mariusnordal.com

Marius Nordal lives in Seattle, Washington with his wife and teenaged daughter. He retired from college teaching after 25 years to spend time writing, composing, sailing and skiing.

He is an unusual musician of many parts. Many know him as "Butch" Nordal, the big band writer who wrote iconic pieces such as "Suncatchers," "Liferaft Earth," and "Oregon." Others know him as a somewhat cutting journalist who has interviewed luminaries such as Keith Jarrett, Chick Corea and Branford Martsalis for *Jazz Times, Downbeat Magazine* and the *Seattle Times*. This journalistic side of his career began suddenly in 2001 after seeing Ken Burns' *Jazz* series on PBS—after which he penned his notorious comedy essay, "Hey Ken, did Baseball end in 1960 too?" Then there is also Nordal the amazing jazz pianist whose three releases on the Origin label have delighted serious jazz fans around the world.

He is currently engaged in various jazz education projects, some of which can now be seen on over 60 videos on YouTube, covering a wide variety of jazz piano topics rarely touched on by others.

SHER MUSIC JAZZ PUBLICATIONS

The Real Easy Book Vol. 1
TUNES FOR BEGINNING IMPROVISERS

Published by Sher Music Co. in conjunction with the Stanford Jazz Workshop. $22 list price.

The easiest tunes from Horace Silver, Eddie Harris, Freddie Hubbard, Red Garland, Sonny Rollins, Cedar Walton, Wes Montgomery Cannonball Adderly, etc. Get yourself or your beginning jazz combo sounding good right away with the first fake book ever designed for the beginning improviser.
Available in C, Bb, Eb and Bass Clef.

The Real Easy Book Vol. 2
TUNES FOR INTERMEDIATE IMPROVISERS

Published by Sher Music Co. in conjunction with the Stanford Jazz Workshop. Over 240 pages. $29.

The best intermediate-level tunes by: Charlie Parker, John Coltrane, Miles Davis, John Scofield, Sonny Rollins, Horace Silver, Wes Montgomery, Freddie Hubbard, Cal Tjader, Cannonball Adderly, and more! Both volumes feature instructional material tailored for each tune. Perfect for jazz combos!
Available in C, Bb, Eb and Bass Clef.

The Real Easy Book Vol. 3
A SHORT HISTORY OF JAZZ

Published by Sher Music Co. in conjunction with the Stanford Jazz Workshop. Over 200 pages. $25.

History text and tunes from all eras and styles of jazz. Perfect for classroom use. Available in C, Bb, Eb and Bass Clef versions.

The Best of Sher Music Co. Real Books
100+ TUNES YOU NEED TO KNOW

A collection of the best-known songs from the world leader in jazz fake books – Sher Music Co.!
Includes songs by: Miles Davis, John Coltrane, Bill Evans, Duke Ellington, Antonio Carlos Jobim, Charlie Parker, John Scofield, Michael Brecker, Weather Report, Horace Silver, Freddie Hubbard, Thelonious Monk, Cannonball Adderley, and many more!

$26. Available in C, Bb, Eb and Bass Clef.

The Serious Jazz Book II
THE HARMONIC APPROACH

By Barry Finnerty, Endorsed by: Joe Lovano, Jamey Aebersold, Hubert Laws, Mark Levine, etc.

- A 200 page, exhaustive study of how to master the harmonic content of songs.
- Contains explanations of every possible type of chord that is used in jazz.
- Clear musical examples to help achieve real harmonic control over melodic improvisation.
- For any instrument. $32. Money back gurantee!

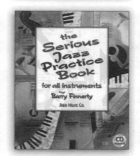

The Serious Jazz Practice Book By Barry Finnerty

A unique and comprehensive plan for mastering the basic building blocks of the jazz language. It takes the most widely-used scales and chords and gives you step-by-step exercises that dissect them into hundreds of cool, useable patterns.
Includes CD - $30 list price.

"The book I've been waiting for!" – Randy Brecker.

"The best book of intervallic studies I've ever seen."
– Mark Levine

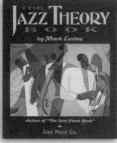

The Jazz Theory Book

By Mark Levine, the most comprehensive Jazz Theory book ever published! $38 list price.
- Over 500 pages of text and over 750 musical examples.
- Written in the language of the working jazz musician, this book is easy to read and user-friendly. At the same time, it is the most comprehensive study of jazz harmony and theory ever published.
- Mark Levine has worked with Bobby Hutcherson, Cal Tjader, Joe Henderson, Woody Shaw, and many other jazz greats.

Jazz Piano Masterclass With Mark Levine
"THE DROP 2 BOOK"

The long-awaited book from the author of "The Jazz Piano Book!" A complete study on how to use "drop 2" chord voicings to create jazz piano magic! 68 pages, plus CD of Mark demonstrating each exercise. $19 list.

"Will make you sound like a real jazz piano player in no time." – Jamey Aebersold

Metaphors For The Musician
By Randy Halberstadt

This practical and enlightening book will help any jazz player or vocalist look at music with "new eyes." Designed for any level of player, on any instrument, "Metaphors For The Musician" provides numerous exercises throughout to help the reader turn these concepts into musical reality.

Guaranteed to help you improve your musicianship. 330 pages – $29 list price. Satisfaction guaranteed!

The Jazz Musicians Guide To Creative Practicing
By David Berkman

Finally a book to help musicians use their practice time wisely! Covers tune analysis, breaking hard tunes into easy components, how to swing better, tricks to playing fast bebop lines, and much more! 150+pages, plus CD. $29 list.

"Fun to read and bursting with things to do and ponder." – Bob Mintzer

The 'Real Easy' Ear Training Book
By Roberta Radley

For all musicians, regardless of instrument or experience, this is the most comprehensive book on "hearing the changes" ever published!
- Covers both beginning and intermediate ear training exercises.
- Music Teachers: You will find this book invaluable in teaching ear training to your students.

Book includes 168 pages of instructional text and musical examples, plus two CDs! $29 list price.

The Jazz Singer's Guidebook By David Berkman

A COURSE IN JAZZ HARMONY AND SCAT SINGING FOR THE SERIOUS JAZZ VOCALIST

A clear, step-by-step approach for serious singers who want to improve their grasp of jazz harmony and gain a deeper understanding of music fundamentals.

This book will change how you hear music and make you a better singer, as well as give you the tools to develop your singing in directions you may not have thought possible.

$26 – includes audio CD demonstrating many exercises.

LATIN MUSIC BOOKS, CDs, DVD

The Latin Real Book (C, Bb or Eb)

The only professional-level Latin fake book ever published!
Over 570 pages. Detailed transcriptions exactly as recorded by:

Ray Barretto	Arsenio Rodriguez	Manny Oquendo	Ivan Lins
Eddie Palmieri	Tito Rodriguez	Puerto Rico All-Stars	Djavan
Fania All-Stars	Orquesta Aragon	Issac Delgaldo	Tom Jobim
Tito Puente	Beny Moré	Ft. Apache Band	Toninho Horta
Ruben Blades	Cal Tjader	Dave Valentin	Joao Bosco
Los Van Van	Andy Narell	Paquito D'Rivera	Milton Nascimento
NG La Banda	Mario Bauza	Clare Fischer	Leila Pinheiro
Irakere	Dizzy Gilllespie	Chick Corea	Gal Costa
Celia Cruz	Mongo Santamaria	Sergio Mendes	**And Many More!**

The Latin Real Book Sampler CD

12 of the greatest Latin Real Book tunes as played by the original artists: Tito Puente, Ray Barretto, Andy Narell, Puerto Rico Allstars, Bacacoto, etc.

$16 list price. Available in U.S.A. only.

The Conga Drummer's Guidebook By Michael Spiro

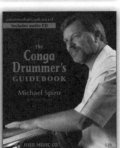

Includes CD - $28 list price. The only method book specifically designed for the intermediate to advanced conga drummer. It goes behind the superficial licks and explains how to approach any Afro-Latin rhythm with the right feel, so you can create a groove like the pros!.

"This book is awesome. Michael is completely knowledgable about his subject."   – Dave Garibaldi

"A breakthrough book for all students of the conga drum."   – Karl Perazzo

Introduction to the Conga Drum - DVD

By Michael Spiro

For beginners, or anyone needing a solid foundation in conga drum technique.

Jorge Alabe – "Mike Spiro is a great conga teacher. People can learn real conga technique from this DVD."

John Santos – "A great musician/teacher who's earned his stripes"

1 hour, 55 minutes running time. $25.

Muy Caliente!

Afro-Cuban Play-Along CD and Book
Rebeca Mauleón - Keyboard
Oscar Stagnaro - Bass
Orestes Vilató - Timbales
Carlos Caro - Bongos
Edgardo Cambon - Congas
Over 70 min. of smokin' Latin grooves!
Stereo separation so you can eliminate the bass or piano. Play-along with a rhythm section featuring some of the top Afro-Cuban musicians in the world! $18.

The True Cuban Bass

By Carlos Del Puerto, (bassist with Irakere) and Silvio Vergara, $22.

For acoustic or electric bass; English and Spanish text; Includes CDs of either historic Cuban recordings or Carlos playing each exercise; Many transcriptions of complete bass parts for tunes in different Cuban styles – the roots of Salsa.

101 Montunos

By Rebeca Mauleón

The only comprehensive study of Latin piano playing ever published.

- Bi-lingual text (English/Spanish)
- 2 CDs of the author demonstrating each montuno
- Covers over 100 years of Afro-Cuban styles, including the danzón, guaracha, mambo, merengue and songo—from Peruchin to Eddie Palmieri. $28

The Salsa Guide Book

By Rebeca Mauleón

The only complete method book on salsa ever published! 260 pages. $25.

Carlos Santana – "A true treasure of knowledge and information about Afro-Cuban music."
Mark Levine, author of The Jazz Piano Book. – "This is the book on salsa."
Sonny Bravo, pianist with Tito Puente – "This will be the salsa 'bible' for years to come."
Oscar Hernández, pianist with Rubén Blades – "An excellent and much needed resource."

The Brazilian Guitar Book

By Nelson Faria, one of Brazil's best new guitarists.

- Over 140 pages of comping patterns, transcriptions and chord melodies for samba, bossa, baiaõ, etc.
- Complete chord voicings written out for each example.
- Comes with a CD of Nelson playing each example.
- The most complete Brazilian guitar method ever published! $28.

Joe Diorio – "Nelson Faria's book is a welcome addition to the guitar literature. I'm sure those who work with this volume wiill benefit greatly"

Inside The Brazilian Rhythm Section

By Nelson Faria and Cliff Korman

This is the first book/CD package ever published that provides an opportunity for bassists, guitarists, pianists and drummers to interact and play-along with a master Brazilian rhythm section. Perfect for practicing both accompanying and soloing.

$28 list price for book and 2 CDs - including the charts for the CD tracks and sample parts for each instrument, transcribed from the recording.

The Latin Bass Book

A PRACTICAL GUIDE
By Oscar Stagnaro

The only comprehensive book ever published on how to play bass in authentic Afro-Cuban, Brazilian, Caribbean, Latin Jazz & South American styles. $34.

Over 250 pages of transcriptions of Oscar Stagnaro playing each exercise. Learn from the best!

Includes: 3 Play-Along CDs to accompany each exercise, featuring world-class rhythm sections.

Afro-Caribbean Grooves for Drumset

By Jean-Philippe Fanfant, drummer with Andy narell's band, Sakesho.

Covers grooves from 10 Caribbean nations, arranged for drumset.

Endorsed by Peter Erskine, Horacio Hernandez, etc.

CD includes both audio and video files. $25.

MORE JAZZ PUBLICATIONS

The Digital Real Book

On the web

Over 850 downloadable tunes from all the Sher Music Co. fakebooks.

See www.shermusic.com for details.

Foundation Exercises for Bass

By Chuck Sher

A creative approach for any style of music, any level, acoustic or electric bass. Perfect for bass teachers!

Filled with hundreds of exercises to help you master scales, chords, rhythms, hand positions, ear training, reading music, sample bass grooves, creating bass lines on common chord progressions, and much more. $24

Jazz Guitar Voicings The Drop 2 Book

By Randy Vincent, Everything you need to know to create full chord melody voicings like Jim Hall, Joe Pass, etc. Luscious voicings for chord melody playing based on the "Drop 2" principle of chord voicings.

You will find that this book covers this essential material in a unique way unlike any other guitar book available.

Endorsed by Julian Lage, John Stowell, Larry Koonse, etc. $25, includes 2 CDs.

Walking Bassics: The Fundamentals of Jazz Bass Playing

By swinging NY bassist Ed Fuqua

Includes transcriptions of every bass note on accompanying CD and step-by-step method for constructing solid walking bass lines. $22.

Endorsed by Eddie Gomez, Jimmy Haslip, John Goldsby, etc.

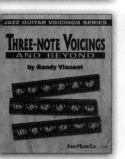

Three-Note Voicings and Beyond

By Randy Vincent, A complete guide to the construction and use of every kind of three-note voicing on guitar.

"Randy Vincent is an extraordinary musician. This book illuminates harmonies in the most sensible and transparent way." – **Pat Metheny**

"This book is full of essential information for jazz guitarists at any level. Wonderful!" – **Mike Stern**

194 pages, $28

Concepts for Bass Soloing

By Chuck Sher and Marc Johnson, (bassist with Bill Evans, etc.) The only book ever published that is specifically designed to improve your soloing! $26

- Includes two CDs of Marc Johnson soloing on each exercise
- Transcriptions of bass solos by: Eddie Gomez, John Patitucci, Scott LaFaro, Jimmy Haslip, etc.

"It's a pleasure to encounter a Bass Method so well conceived and executed." – **Steve Swallow**

The Jazz Piano Book

By Mark Levine, Concord recording artist and pianist with Cal Tjader. For beginning to advanced pianists. The only truly comprehensive method ever published! Over 300 pages. $32

Richie Beirach –"The best new method book available."
Hal Galper – "This is a must!"
Jamey Aebersold – "This is an invaluable resource for any pianist."
James Williams – "One of the most complete anthologies on jazz piano."
Also available in Spanish! ¡El Libro del Jazz Piano!

The Improvisor's Bass Method

By Chuck Sher. A complete method for electric or acoustic bass, plus transcribed solos and bass lines by Mingus, Jaco, Ron Carter, Scott LaFaro, Paul Jackson, Ray Brown, and more! Over 200 pages. $16

International Society of Bassists – "Undoubtedly the finest book of its kind."
Eddie Gomez – "Informative, readily comprehensible and highly imaginative"

The Blues Scales

ESSENTIAL TOOLS FOR JAZZ IMPROVISATION
By Dan Greenblatt

Great Transcriptions from Miles, Dizzy Gillespie, Lester Young, Oscar Peterson, Dave Sanborn, Michael Brecker and many more, showing how the Blues Scales are actually used in various styles of jazz.

Accompanying CD by author Dan Greenblatt and his swinging quartet of New York jazz musicians shows how each exercise should sound. And it also gives the student numerous play-along tracks to practice with. $22

Essential Grooves

FOR WRITING, PERFORMING AND PRODUCING CONTEMPORARY MUSIC
By 3 Berklee College professors: Dan Moretti, Matthew Nicholl and Oscar Stagnaro

- 41 different rhythm section grooves used in Soul, Rock, Motown, Funk, Hip-hop, Jazz, Afro-Cuban, Brazilian, music and more!
- Includes CD and multi-track DVD with audio files to create play-alongs, loops, original music, and more. $24

Forward Motion

FROM BACH TO BEBOP
A Corrective Approach to Jazz Phrasing
By Hal Galper

- Perhaps the most important jazz book in a decade, Forward Motion shows the reader how to create jazz phrases that swing with authentic jazz feeling.
- Hal Galper was pianist with Cannonball Adderley, Phil Woods, Stan Getz, Chet Baker, John Scofield, and many other jazz legends.
- Each exercise available on an interactive website so that the reader can change tempos, loop the exercises, transpose them, etc. $30.

The World's Greatest Fake Book

Jazz & Fusion Tunes by: **Coltrane, Mingus, Jaco, Chick Corea, Bird, Herbie Hancock, Bill Evans, McCoy, Beirach, Ornette, Wayne Shorter, Zawinul, AND MANY MORE!** $32

Chick Corea – "Great for any students of jazz.'
Dave Liebman – "The fake book of the 80's."
George Cables – "The most carefully conceived fake book I've ever seen."